# INTERNET LEARNING AND THE BUILDING OF KNOWLEDGE

# INTERNET LEARNING AND THE BUILDING OF KNOWLEDGE

*Juliann Cortese*

CAMBRIA
PRESS

YOUNGSTOWN, NEW YORK

Library of Congress Cataloging-in-Publication Data
Cortese, Juliann
    Internet learning and the building of knowledge / Juliann Cortese.
        p. cm.
    Includes bibliographical references and index.
    ISBN 978-1-934043-13-4 (alk. paper)
    1. Social psychology. 2. Cognition—Social aspects. 3. Internet—Social aspects.
4. Web sites—Design. 5. Communication in medicine. I. Title.

    HM1033.C675 2007
    303.48'34—dc22

2007006340

*Dedicated to Joelie (my heart),
John (my soul), Claire (my courage),
and Joe (my determination)*

# TABLE OF CONTENTS

List of Figures ................................................................. xiii

List of Tables................................................................. xvi

Foreword ..................................................................... xix

Preface........................................................................ xxv

Acknowledgments........................................................ xxix

Chapter One: Study One: Introduction / Overview of Study Goals ........ 1

    Social Cognitive Theory ............................................... 2

        Behavior / Learning................................................ 4

        Environment / Hypermedia ................................... 17

        Personal Factors / Human Agency ......................... 32

    Study Design........................................................... 42

Chapter Two: Method ........................................................ 45

    Procedure ................................................................ 45

    Stimulus ................................................................. 46

Sample ........................................................................................... 51

    Age ......................................................................................... 51

    Gender ................................................................................... 51

    Race ....................................................................................... 51

    Class Rank ............................................................................ 52

    Marital Status ....................................................................... 52

    Income .................................................................................. 52

Measures ...................................................................................... 53

    Moderator / Independent Variables ................................... 53

    Dependent Variables ............................................................ 57

Data Analysis .............................................................................. 58

Chapter Three: Results ............................................................... 59

Preliminary Relationships .......................................................... 59

Manipulation Check .................................................................... 60

    Definitional Manipulation Check ...................................... 60

    Relational Manipulation Check .......................................... 61

Site Design Manipulation and Knowledge ................................ 61

Definitional Knowledge and Site Design .............................. 61

Knowledge Structure Density and Site Design .................... 63

Factual Knowledge and Site Design ..................................... 63

Subject Expertise ...................................................................... 64

Definitional Knowledge and Subject Expertise..................... 64

Knowledge Structure Density and Subject Expertise............ 65

Factual Knowledge and Subject Expertise ............................ 66

Web Expertise ........................................................................... 67

Definitional Knowledge and Web Expertise ......................... 67

Knowledge Structure Density and Web Expertise ................ 68

Factual Knowledge and Web Expertise................................. 69

Motivation ................................................................................. 69

Definitional Knowledge and Motivation .............................. 69

Knowledge Structure Density and Motivation...................... 70

Factual Knowledge and Motivation ...................................... 71

Internet Self-Efficacy ................................................................. 72

   Definitional Knowledge and Internet Self-Efficacy .............. 72

   Knowledge Structure Density and Internet Self-Efficacy ..... 73

   Factual Knowledge and Internet Self-Efficacy ..................... 74

Cognitive Load ........................................................................... 74

   Definitional Knowledge and Cognitive Load ....................... 74

   Knowledge Structure Density and Cognitive Load ............... 77

   Factual Knowledge and Cognitive Load ............................... 79

Overall Main Effects Models ..................................................... 79

   Definitional Knowledge ....................................................... 79

   Knowledge Structure Density .............................................. 82

   Factual Knowledge .............................................................. 82

Chapter Four: Discussion ........................................................... 85

Basic Relationships Between Variables ...................................... 85

Manipulation Checks .................................................................. 87

Site Design and Knowledge ........................................................ 88

Subject Expertise ............................................................... 90

Web Expertise .................................................................. 91

Motivation ...................................................................... 92

Internet Self-Efficacy...................................................... 94

Cognitive Load ............................................................... 95

Factors Affecting Knowledge .......................................... 96

Limitations...................................................................... 97

Future Research .............................................................. 99

Chapter Five: Study Two ................................................ 101

Method............................................................................ 103

    Procedure.................................................................... 103

    Stimulus..................................................................... 105

    Sample........................................................................ 105

    Measures..................................................................... 107

Data Analysis.................................................................. 109

Results ............................................................................ 109

Preliminary Relationships ................................................. 109

Pre / Post-Knowledge Structure Density ............................ 110

Personal Factors and Knowledge Structure Density ........... 114

Discussion................................................................. 114

Preliminary Relationships ................................................. 114

Pre / Post-Knowledge Structure Density ............................ 116

Independent Variables and Post-Knowledge
Structure Density................................................................ 118

Limitations............................................................... 119

Future Research ........................................................ 120

Overall Conclusions ................................................. 121

Appendix A: Study One Instructions ............................. 125

Appendix B: Study One Questionnaire............................ 126

Appendix C: Study Two Instructions............................. 146

Appendix D: Study Two Questionnaire........................... 148

References................................................................ 167

Name Index............................................................. 177

Subject Index ........................................................... 181

# LIST OF FIGURES

Figure 1. Overall Theoretical Model of Study One ............................. 4

Figure 2. Study Design Model ............................................................. 43

Figure 3. Stimulus Webpage Topic Structure ..................................... 47

Figure 4. Sample Page, Basic Site ...................................................... 48

Figure 5. Sample Page, Definitional Site ............................................ 49

Figure 6. Sample Page, Relational Site ............................................... 50

Figure 7. Histogram of Web Expertise
(Days of Web Use from the Prior Week) ............................. 54

Figure 8. Histogram of Web Expertise
(1–10, Novice to Expert Rating) ......................................... 55

Figure 9. Significant Difference Between the Definitional
and Relational Sites for Definitional Knowledge
(Hypothesis 1a) ................................................................... 62

Figure 10. Significant Difference Between the Basic
and Relational Sites for Factual Knowledge
(Research Question 1) ........................................................ 64

Figure 11. Estimated Marginal Means for Definitional
Knowledge by Site Condition, Accounting
for Subject Expertise (Hypothesis 2a) ............................... 66

Figure 12. Estimated Marginal Means for Definitional
Knowledge by Site Condition, Accounting
for Web Expertise (Hypothesis 3a) .................................... 68

Figure 13. Estimated Marginal Means for Definitional
Knowledge by Site Condition, Accounting
for Motivation (Hypothesis 4) .......................................... 70

Figure 14. Interaction Between Motivation
and Site Condition for Knowledge Structure Density ...... 72

Figure 15. Estimated Marginal Means for Definitional
Knowledge by Site Condition, Accounting
for Internet Self-Efficacy (Hypothesis 5) ........................ 73

Figure 16. Estimated Marginal Means for Definitional
Knowledge by Site Condition, Accounting
for Cognitive Load–Effort (Hypothesis 6a) ..................... 75

Figure 17. Interaction Between Cognitive Load
(Misunderstanding) and Site Condition
for Definitional Knowledge ............................................. 77

Figure 18. Estimated Marginal Means for Definitional
Knowledge by Site Condition, Accounting for all
Control Variables (Overall Model Containing CLE) ........ 80

Figure 19. Estimated Marginal Means for Definitional
Knowledge by Site Condition, Accounting for all
Control Variables (Overall Model Containing CLM) ....... 81

Figure 20. Solomon Four-Group Design used in Study Two........... 104

Figure 21. Solomon Four-Group Analysis Results .......................... 112

Figure 22. Interaction Between Stimulus and Pretest
in Predicting Knowledge Structure Density ................... 113

# LIST OF TABLES

Table 1. Study One Correlation Table ............................................... 60

Table 2. Raw Means for Knowledge Measures
Across Site Conditions .......................................................... 63

Table 3. Mean Knowledge Structure Density Scores
for the Site Condition / Motivation Interaction ................... 71

Table 4. Mean Definitional Knowledge Scores
for the Site Condition / Cognitive
Load (Misunderstanding) Interaction ................................... 77

Table 5. Definitional Knowledge Overall Model of Effects,
Including Cognitive Load (Effort) ........................................ 81

Table 6. Definitional Knowledge Overall Model of Effects,
Including Cognitive Load (Misunderstanding) .................... 82

Table 7. Knowledge Structure Density Overall Model
of Effects, Including Cognitive Load (Effort) ...................... 82

Table 8. Knowledge Structure Density Overall Model of Effects,
Including Cognitive Load (Misunderstanding) .................... 83

Table 9. Factual Knowledge Overall Model of Effects,
Including Cognitive Load (Effort) ........................................ 83

Table 10. Factual Knowledge Overall Model of Effects,
Including Cognitive Load (Misunderstanding) .................. 83

Table 11. Study Two Correlations Between all Variables
and Post-Knowledge Structure Density Using
the Whole Sample and each Experimental Condition...... 110

Table 12. Study Two Independent Variable Correlation Table .........111

Table 13. Multiple Regression for Variables Predicting
Knowledge Structure Density ......................................... 115

# FOREWORD

It is not exaggeration to say that the Internet has changed the way people in the United States get information about any number of topics, from politics and public affairs to health and diet information. But change happens slowly, and it takes time for practitioners and researchers to understand how to fully utilize the potential of a new medium. For instance, early television news was really little more than radio news with a camera aimed at the talking head. It was some time before television news began to truly take advantage of the visual nature of the television medium, and in many ways television news continues to this day to develop with the use of crawling text and modified news formats. Newspapers, too, have adapted their form and content in response to the competition from television news. Whether these changes are for the better or worse is a topic for another time and place, but the change itself is undeniable.

Recent survey research by the Pew Internet and American Life Project found that, among those with Internet access (currently over 70%

of the U.S. adult population), more than half of individuals helping to care for someone with a major illness considered information found online to be their most important source of information. Even a quarter of the individuals who deal with their own major health problems said the Internet plays either a major or at least important role. But, how effective is the Internet, and in particular the World Wide Web, in communicating health information to the public? Public perceptions of the value of information aside, is the Web truly valuable in this domain, and even if it is, can it be designed to become even more valuable?

In this volume, Juliann Cortese takes up the task of understanding the potential of the Web to provide information to the public on the topic of health, in particular the burgeoning area of alternative medicine. As with television news, much of the health-related information available on the Web since its inception a little over a decade ago has taken a form little different from prior forms of mediated information like television and magazines. Designers and practitioners are still trying to find the best way to use the interactive nature of the Web to most effectively convey information to those who need it. Although the creativity of designers may present new approaches, any design advances should be tested through formative and evaluative research to assess their contribution. Too many supposed improvements in other media have led to actually detrimental effects.

Cortese's approach begins with a focus on theories of human cognition, information processing, and learning to anticipate ways in which the Web can be used to improve upon prior approaches communicating health information. She identifies the use of pop-up windows as a means to convey information to encourage understanding of word definitions and the relationships among related concepts in a text. These "definitional" and "relational" site designs play to the strength of the Web and its interactive nature—providing just the right information at just the time it is needed but otherwise not allowing it to distract from the primary text. Cortese then compares learning of basic facts, definitions, and "knowledge structure density[1]" across basic, definitional, and relational site designs. The findings, however, are not as initially expected.

Based on the results of the first, well-controlled study, Cortese finds that the relational site appears to actually *inhibit* definitional knowledge gain compared to the other two site designs. The design of the site—initially, at least—also appears to have no influence on the other two forms of knowledge. Combining across a number of tests with various levels of statistical control, one could conclude that the best overall site design would be the definitional site design because it increased definitional knowledge (compared to the relational site) but did not appear to inhibit either factual learning or knowledge structure density.

However, the story is more complicated than this. In fact the effectiveness of the relational site is dependent upon the user's level of motivation. Among those highly motivated (and the likely real-world users of such a health site), the relational site is considerably better at encouraging knowledge structure density than its basic and definitional competitors. Those who are generally least motivated, do worst at increasing knowledge structure from exposure to the relational site. This appears to be further evidence that there is often an interaction between user characteristics and media attributes or design—similar to what educational technologists have called the "aptitude-treatment interaction" and communication researchers have studied under the "knowledge gap hypothesis"—that makes it impossible to offer a "one size fits all" design solution that will optimize results for all users.

---

[1] Knowledge structure density is conceptualized as the extent to which individuals see concepts within a domain as related to one another (vs. failing to see relationships among ostensibly related concepts).

Following up on this first study and its somewhat unanticipated findings, Cortese employs the venerable Solomon Four-Group Design to better isolate the effects of use of the basic site design on knowledge structure density. In a finding consistent with her first study, Cortese demonstrates that in the posttest component of the Solomon Four-Group Design, simple exposure to the basic site design does not appear to enhance knowledge structure density compared to individuals who are not exposed to the site. However, in what might be downplayed as merely a demonstration of a threat to the external validity of a pretest and posttest experimental design for this type of research, Cortese finds that among those who were given the knowledge structure density measure in both pretest and posttest, density increases among those exposed to the basic site. That is, the basic site increases knowledge structure density only among those who have been exposed to the pretest, or what Campbell and Stanley refer to as "sensitization." Rather than simply chalking this finding up to an anomaly of experimental design, Cortese offers an interesting theoretical account of this effect and its implications for site design. She theorizes that the pretest primed participants to focus attention on the information implicitly being conveyed by basic hyperlinks in the Web site. When encouraged to think about how concepts are related via this sort of priming, everyday hyperlinks can in fact encourage individuals to increase their knowledge structure density. This second study, then, sheds light on another mechanism—beyond the relational site design of Study One—that might be used to encourage one aspect of learning from online health information.

This book falls at the fruitful intersection of technology design, cognitive psychology, education, and communication. Cortese moves deftly through the literatures in each of these fields to design and execute two clean studies that help to advance our understanding of the complex interplay between human motivation, information processing, educational technology design, and learning. It moves the literature in this exciting and pragmatic domain forward and demonstrates where the next phase of research should go.

Dr. William P. Eveland, Jr.
Associate Professor of Communication & Political Science
School of Communication
The Ohio State University

# PREFACE

The focus of the research reported here was on basic World Wide Web content and the examination of ways to help individuals learn this content while browsing. As such, issues relating to online classes and distance learning were beyond the scope of this particular research. Learning was examined through basic recall as well as knowledge structure—the meaningful connections individuals make between concepts. The more connections we make between concepts, the more tightly they are held in our memory and the denser our knowledge structure. Two studies were undertaken for this research: Pop-up previews attached to hyperlinks were part of the experimental manipulation for study one and knowledge structure change after exposure was the focus of study two.

Since the completion of this study in May 2005, research has progressed in this area. The following provides a current review of the relevant research.

Maes, van Geel, and Cozijn (2006) examined the use of previews in the hypermedia environment. They created three versions of a website, one without previews and two with previews attached to hyperlinks.

The two experimental conditions differed slightly in the content of the previews—one focused on descriptive information (semantic) and the other on user information (pragmatic). Site content focused on a new cell phone, so the semantic previews contained information about the phone and the pragmatic previews instructed readers how to use the features of the phone. Findings of the study revealed that the previews helped users to navigate more efficiently but did not significantly impact user effectiveness during a search task or user evaluation of website usability.

Although Maes, et al. (2006) used previews in their study, there are key differences between their methods and those reported here. The previews in the research reported here were pop-up windows that covered part of the webpage text, whereas Maes, et al. used a preview pane in a stationary location. Also, the study reported here focused on relational and definitional information as preview content, whereas Maes, et al. examined semantic and pragmatic information. These differences are important to consider because they reveal that more research is needed to understand the use of previews in the learning process both in terms of web structure and content.

Other recent studies have focused on related issues of hypermedia learning that have been discussed previously in the literature such as navigational organization and linear versus nonlinear representations.

For instance, Trumpower and Goldsmith (2004) examined three navigational organization patterns: expert (nonlinear design, but influenced by the knowledge structure of an expert), random (nonlinear design, but without expert guidance), and alphabetical (linear design). They found that those who used the expert navigational structure acquired superior knowledge structures (examined using definitional and conceptual knowledge assessments) of their own and went on to perform better in a related task.

On the other hand, Lee, Tedder, and Xie (2006) examined linear and nonlinear presentations of three types of text: blocked (independent elements of the whole), ordered (required reading from beginning to end for comprehension) and detailed layered (each fact followed by sufficient detail with main and subpoints). Their findings differed based on the amount of working memory available for each individual. In general they noted that individuals with low working memory acquired higher recall scores when reading the linear scrolling text than when reading the hyperlinked, paged text for two of the three text formats examined. The researchers provided full details of several interactions found in their study.

As indicated by the research reported in this book and by the studies presented here, there is much to be done to fully understand learning in the hypermedia environment and how to enhance that learning. If we are to assume that a primary function of the Internet is to provide information, then we must continue to examine ways to maximize its effectiveness in this area.

## REFERENCES

Lee, M. J., Tedder, M. C., & Xie, G. (2006). Effective computer text design to enhance readers' recall: Text formats, individual working memory capacity and content type. *Journal of Technical Writing and Communication, 36*, 57–73.

Maes, A., van Geel, A., & Cozijn, R. (2006). Signposts on the digital highway: The effect of semantic and pragmatic hyperlink previews. *Interacting with Computers, 18*, 265–282.

Trumpower, D. L., & Goldsmith, T. E. (2004). Structural enhancement of learning. *Contemporary Educational Psychology, 29*, 426–446.

# ACKNOWLEDGMENTS

I wish to thank William P. Eveland, Jr. for his guidance, insight, and patience throughout my time at The Ohio State University. Chip has been a mentor and a friend, guiding me through my development as a researcher, teacher, and valuable member of the academic community. I also wish to thank Prabu David for his expertise and support. Prabu's ongoing influence and nurturing have been elemental to my development in the field. Thanks also to Matthew S. Eastin, who helped me to view media use theories from a different perspective. His influence in this area has been extremely valuable.

I thank Anthony Paul for his web design advice, Joe Szymczak and Robb Hagen for their help regarding server access and questionnaire management, and Phil Smith for his help in elevating my awareness of user-centered design.

I am also very grateful to have had a dedicated support network of family and friends. Special thanks to my daughter, Joelie Campana, for being so sweet and agreeable; my husband, John Campana, for keeping me grounded and focused; my parents, Joseph and Claire Cortese, for the exorbitant amount of time they have volunteered to the cause; my parents-in-law, Gene and Cathy Campana, for their prayers and support; and my aunt, Noreen Sozio, for always being there to listen. Special thanks also to dear friends: Michael Marshall, for his encouragement and advice; Catherine Gynn, for her empathetic words of wisdom; Mihye Seo, for inspiring me to do my best; and D'Arcy John Oaks and Len Cooper for their friendship and support.

# INTERNET LEARNING AND THE BUILDING OF KNOWLEDGE

# CHAPTER ONE

# STUDY ONE: INTRODUCTION / OVERVIEW OF STUDY GOALS

Bandura (2002a) has suggested a strong link between health communication and technology by pointing out the active role patients can take in pursuing their health concerns. He indicated that the conception of health has shifted recently from a disease model to a health model, placing more emphasis on goals to stay healthy than means for curing diseases. In response, new technologies can be helpful tools for management of health choices and behaviors. For instance, research has indicated that HIV positive individuals turned to Internet resources to acquire information about their disease (Kalichman, et al., 2003) and used the information during meetings with their health care providers (Kalichman, et al., 2002).

Cassell, Jackson, and Cheuvront (1998) pointed out the hybrid nature of the Internet in the area of health communication. They suggested that the Internet shares characteristics of both mass and interpersonal communication channels. As a mass medium, it has broad reach and utilizes audio and visual formats to display information. As an interpersonal channel it provides an opportunity for interactivity and feedback between individuals. Although both channels make the Internet a prime resource for health information, it is the use of the World Wide Web (WWW) for health information seeking that is of interest in the current study.

The research presented here utilizes Social Cognitive Theory (SCT) as a theoretical basis. SCT provides a structure for the research, but this study is not an examination of the theory itself.

SCT suggests that one's behaviors, personal factors, and environment interact and provide the individual with control over his / her life (Bandura, 1986). When applying SCT to a learning context, key factors emerge such as web and subject expertise, motivation, self-efficacy, and environmental factors. The purpose of this research is to understand better the learning process as it relates to information acquired through the WWW. Health-related information on the WWW provides a specific context within which to examine this type of information retrieval and use.

Literature from several different areas is presented in order to examine background information for this study. The structure and focus of the literature review is based on the three major elements of Social Cognitive Theory (behavior, the environment, and personal factors) and how they provide a theoretical basis for the examination of learning from the WWW.

## SOCIAL COGNITIVE THEORY

Social Cognitive Theory provides a theoretical basis for the examination of Internet learning, as well as health information seeking. SCT places emphasis on control of one's life through a triadic reciprocal set of relationships linking behaviors, cognitive and personal factors, and the environment (Bandura, 1986). These elements influence one another and guide the choices that we make. Furthermore, they provide a basis for understanding human behavior. The cognitive and personal factors element of SCT refers to the personal characteristics of individuals. An overarching element of SCT that can be associated with personal characteristics is Bandura's notion of human agency (Bandura, 2001). There are four features of human agency: intentionality, forethought, self-reactivity, and self-reflection. Intentionality is an active effort to engage in some form of activity; that is, events happen by choice, because we make them happen. Forethought entails planning to achieve certain outcomes. Self-reactivity refers to self-regulatory capabilities such as motivation and goal setting. Finally, self-reflection is our ability to examine and evaluate our thoughts and actions. A key component of self-reflection is self-efficacy. Self-efficacy is an individual's belief that s/he is capable of successfully completing a task. Bandura refers to self-efficacy as the foundation of human agency (Bandura, 2001, 2002b). Self-efficacy is especially important in the health information arena in that people with high self-efficacy toward their health goals can succeed with little intervention; however, those with low self-efficacy will require more guidance (Bandura, 2002a).

Turning to the second element in the triadic relationship, it is part of human nature to seek to understand our environment. In order to facilitate this need we often turn to a variety of communication channels including interpersonal and mediated channels. The Internet is a tempting tool to satisfy our informational needs, especially as they relate to health information. Similarly, SCT can be helpful in understanding the connection between learning and hypermedia use.

Finally, for the last element in the triadic relationship, the behavior of interest in this study is learning. Learning can be viewed as a process in which individuals receive information and then store it for later retrieval. An important strategy that may influence the learning process is elaboration, which encourages in-depth processing of encountered information.

FIGURE 1.    Overall Theoretical Model of Study One

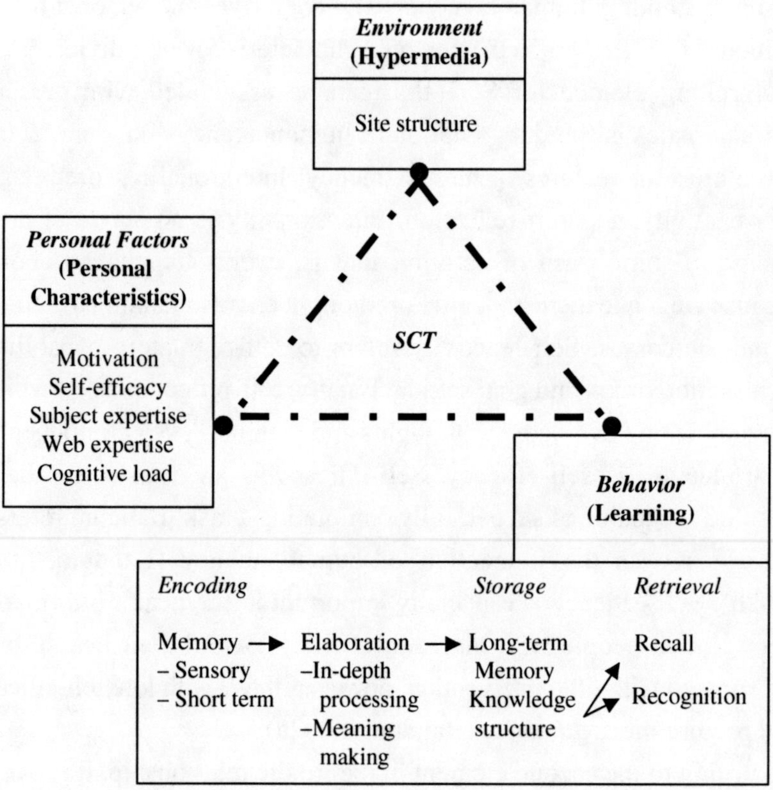

**Environment**
**(Hypermedia)**

Site structure

**Personal Factors**
**(Personal**
**Characteristics)**

Motivation
Self-efficacy
Subject expertise
Web expertise
Cognitive load

*SCT*

**Behavior**
**(Learning)**

| Encoding | | Storage | Retrieval |
|---|---|---|---|
| Memory → | Elaboration → | Long-term | Recall |
| – Sensory | –In-depth | Memory | |
| – Short term | processing | Knowledge | Recognition |
| | –Meaning | structure | |
| | making | | |

Figure 1 portrays the conceptual framework of this study using elements of SCT and literature related to learning processes. The elements of SCT (behavior, environment, and personal factors) will serve as a framework for presentation of pertinent literature relating to learning from the WWW.

*Behavior / Learning*

As stated earlier, the basis of SCT is grounded in the triadic reciprocal relationship between personal factors, the environment, and behaviors. The behavior of interest in this study is learning. Issues related to learning in general and learning from the WWW are addressed in the following sections.

Learning Theories

Three classes of learning theories have proven helpful in understanding the learning process: behavioral, cognitive, and constructivist theories. Each varies in the way learning is conceptualized (Schunk, 2000; see also Ertmer & Newby, 1993). For instance, the behaviorist view defines learning as a change in the frequency or type of behavior. Focus is placed on the stimulus / response nature of learning.

Cognitive theorists place less emphasis on the actions of learners and more on what individuals know and how they acquire that knowledge. The focus of this perspective is placed on information acquisition, organization, storage, and retrieval. Both the behaviorist and cognitivist views consider the environment to be a strong factor in influencing learning. Cognitive theorists also acknowledge the importance of learner characteristics such as abilities, attitudes, and beliefs. For example, a learner must feel competent in his / her ability to learn in order to succeed.

The constructivist view suggests that learning is achieved through the construction of meaning based on experiences. The learner and environment are both important factors; however, constructivists view the interaction between the two as the important issue. The context within which learning occurs is a primary focus in this view. Another important factor in the constructivist perspective is that learning is an involved and intentional activity that requires that learners have an intention to learn, actively process material, and reflect on the material studied (Jonassen, Hernandez-Serrano, & Choi, 2000). Constructivists view learning as an intentional activity in which individuals make sense out of the world around them. Often an individual will encounter some type of dissonance or question that needs to be resolved and they will seek out information to answer the question or resolve the dissonance encountered. Therefore, learning is seen as goal directed and intentional.

It should be mentioned here that, although learning is viewed as intentional in the research detailed here, learning is not always active or intentional. Although we may set out to solve a particular dilemma or question, often we will encounter other information that is useful, but not related to the question at hand. Incidental learning happens when we find information that answers a secondary or previously posed question (Hess, 1999). Though not intentionally sought, this new information would be incorporated into our mental model the same way that intentionally sought information would be applied. Postman (1964) defined incidental learning as occurring when learning is not intended and indicated that there is no need to make a distinction between incidental and intentional learning as they are both based on the same underlying principles.

The Learning Process

Memory is the central mechanism in the learning process, such that all information encountered by an individual is encoded, stored, and retrieved from memory. Therefore, although *learning* may be the process of encoding, storage, and retrieval of information, *memory* is the processor that makes it possible.

There has been a great deal of research on memory, from defining memory to understanding its structure and mechanisms. In attempts to define memory, several definitions and types of memory have emerged. For instance, iconic memory is the storage of brief visual displays (Sperling, 1960). Also, episodic memory is based on past experiences, whereas semantic memory is based on meanings created through knowledge of symbols, concepts, and rules of interpretation (Tulving, 1972). Specifically, semantic memory is a memory model in which nodes are connected by associative links, which are based on meanings (Quillian, 1968). Through these interconnections, further meaning is derived, which goes beyond a simple word definition to the full concept embodied by the word.

Memory has also been defined in terms of how it is structured. Traditionally, a multi-store model of memory has been widely accepted among scholars. Long-term (LTM) and short-term memory (STM) are generally considered to be two forms of storage in such a model. Typically short-term memory is considered to have a limited capacity of about seven, plus or minus, two items (Miller, 1956), and it serves as a storage space for processing information (Glanzer, 1972). Long-term memory, on the other hand is a storage space where more information is held for a considerably longer time. Although STM and LTM are often considered to be two separate storage spaces, researchers have also argued that they can be viewed as elements on a continuum (Melton, 1963) and that information can often be held in both stores simultaneously (Waugh & Norman, 1965).

The Atkinson–Shiffrin (A–S) model is one of the most well known models of human memory from a multi-store perspective. Atkinson and Shiffrin drew on the earlier work of Broadbent and Neisser who also suggested multi-store systems of memory (Lachman, Lachman, & Butterfield, 1979). Similarly, Waugh and Norman's (1965) memory model is also a precursor to the A–S model. Waugh and Norman suggested a two-store model distinguishing between long-term and short-term memory by discussing them as *primary* and *secondary* memory (these terms were originally used by James, 1890, as indicated in Waugh & Norman, 1965). The model outlined a process whereby rehearsal of information in the limited primary store could transfer that information into the larger and more stable secondary store. It should be noted here that although the A–S model is not the first multi-store model, it is a very heavily cited model in experimental psychology (Izawa, 1999).

The Atkinson and Shiffrin model is a three-part memory model consisting of the sensory register, the short-term store and the long-term store (Atkinson & Shiffrin, 1968). The sensory register receives auditory and visual stimuli through our senses. The short-term store (STS; also referred to as the working memory) is where information is held before it is either lost or transferred into the long-term store (LTS). Information enters the STS from both the sensory register and the LTS. Newly acquired information enters the sensory register and then moves to the STS for processing and possible further storage in the LTS. Within the STS is a rehearsal buffer that holds items while they are rehearsed for long term storage. Similarly, when asked to retrieve information from the LTS, this information will enter the STS for processing and possible usage as a response. Here, information retrieved is compared to the requested information criteria and either a response is generated or the search through the LTS continues. Within the LTS, control processes work to store and retrieve information (Atkinson & Shiffrin, 1968; Shiffrin & Atkinson, 1969). Control processes are individual decisions we make when processing information. Within the storage process, we determine what information to store, how to store it, where to store it in terms of placement, and what proportion of information to store. Within the retrieval process we activate a search for information in the LTS, recover that information to the STS, analyze the information recovered, and either generate a response or continue the search. Decay of information can happen at all stages of this model. Atkinson and Shiffrin (1968) addressed forgetting by suggesting that information can be either destroyed, making retrieval impossible, or damaged, in that retrieval may be delayed temporarily or permanently.

Both Atkinson and Shiffrin have proposed updated versions of the A–S model. For instance, the Atkinson–Joula theory maintains the basic three-store system, but adds information to the model in the areas of coding, long-term memory substores, and memory scanning tasks (Lachman, et al., 1979). They expressed coding as perceptual and conceptual; they further divided the LTS into episodic and semantic memory; and they expand the process of retrieval from LTS by explaining memory scanning in further detail. The Shiffrin–Schneider theory, on the other hand, suggests major revisions to the model and attempts to connect selective attention to the scanning of memory for information retrieval. They apply automatic detection and controlled search processes to both attention and memory scanning. Automatic detection processes are unconscious and rely on previously experienced search routines; and controlled search processes are deliberate and have a specific sequence of steps. Shiffrin was also involved in proposing the Search of Asso-ciative Memory (SAM) model (Raaijmakers & Shiffrin, 1981). The SAM places more focus on the LTS than the original A–S model. Issues related to storage and retrieval are stressed in this model including the storage of an image of the perceived stimulus, storage based on relationships between items, and the use of retrieval cues to recall items from the LTS (Estes, 1999).

In opposition to the multi-store approach, researchers have suggested other views of the memory process. Donald Norman, a cognitive psychologist who has contributed greatly to memory theory, has rejected multi-store models, focusing the majority of his work on the content and structure of long-term memory (Lachman, et al., 1979). He suggests that short-term memory is not a separate entity, but part of the long-term storage process. Alternatives to the multi-store model include analogue memory, which is memory for perceptual events that are usually in the form of a visual display. Analogue memory is usually associated with issues related to mental imagery and multiple coding of stimuli.

Another alternative is encoding specificity, which is the notion that a target item can be remembered more easily when it is learned and retrieved using the same cues (Lachman, et al., 1979). Initial research in this area suggested that recall was higher in a cued condition than when using noncued recall (Tulving & Pearlstone, 1966). Taking this a step further, research has indicated that retrieval cue words must be presented with target words at the time of learning in order to enhance recall of the target word (Tulving & Osler, 1968). Furthermore, one retrieval cue is sufficient as experiments utilizing two cues were no more effective when compared to single cues. Even free recall experiments have indicated that highly related words will be retrieved from memory as single units (Tulving & Patterson, 1968). Highly related words are presented as a block together within a list of terms. This unitization was displayed when highly associated words were placed at both the middle and end of a list; however, higher unitization of terms was displayed when associated words were placed at the end of a list.

The levels of processing approach is another alternative to the multi-store memory view (Lachman, et al., 1979). Craik and Lockhart (1972) have supported a levels of processing approach in which information processing is presented as a hierarchy of stages. They suggest that *depth of processing* can aid learning. The depth that they refer to is the focus of semantic and cognitive analysis used to process newly acquired information.

The preceding discussion is not meant to provide a history of memory models, but instead it should serve as a brief background review of some of the research on memory. Certainly there are many other models and theories that have been proposed including Morton's (1970) Logogen model, Murdock's (1972) Finite-State Decision Model, Murdock's (1982, 1999) Theory of Distributed Associative Memory (TODAM), the Linear Association Model (LAM), Spreading-Activation theory, MINERVA2, the Composite Holographic Associative Recall Model (CHARM), the Resonance-Retrieval Model (see Murdock, 1999 for a description and full citation of the five preceding models / theories), the Array Model, MINERVA, Matched Filters, Matrix, and Resonance (see Estes, 1999 for a description and full citation of the five preceding models / theories). The important point to consider is that many of the multi-store models promote the basic memory processes of encoding, storage, and retrieval. But, as stipulated by alternative approaches (i.e., depth of processing) it is important to consider the cognitive process of meaning making.

In her Limited Capacity Model, Lang (2000) took much of this prior research into consideration when constructing this model that addresses the processing of mediated messages. As learning from the WWW entails information processing of mediated messages, it is suited to examination under the guidelines of this model. The two main assumptions of the model are that people inherently process information and that their information processing ability is limited due to the capacity of their processing resources. Lang suggested that messages may not be processed fully because individuals do not choose to allocate enough resources to the task or may have fewer resources available than are necessary to complete the task. A reflection of prior research provides the background for a model composed of three subprocesses that are believed to occur simultaneously: encoding, storage, and retrieval.

The first subprocess is encoding and it refers to the receipt of information from the environment (Lang, 2000). The encoding subprocess can be further divided into two steps. First, information is encoded into sensory receptors (eyes, ears, nose, mouth, and skin). Second, the information moves into short-term memory where it is transformed into mental representations. This encoding stage is closely linked with the retrieval stage because the ways in which information is perceived at the encoding stage determine how / what is stored. Appropriate retrieval cues can then be chosen depending on what and how information is stored. (Tulving & Thomson, 1973).

The storage subprocess is the organization of ones' memory into an associative network of links (Lang, 2000). New information is held more firmly in storage when more associative links are created. This storage subprocess is basically what has been described earlier as long-term memory or semantic memory. The important component to consider is that information is stored based on its meaningful relationships to other pieces of information. For instance, schema theory provides a theoretical description of how individuals organize information and create meanings (Jonassen, Beissner, & Yacci, 1993). Schemas contain slots of information that when organized appropriately can be combined to describe particular objects, events, and ideas. Furthermore, schemas can connect to one another to provide meaningful relationships among pieces of information. Learning is the process by which we structure and restructure these connections (Jonassen, 1988, 1993; Jonassen, et al., 1993). Learning is viewed as a process because it is continuous meaning making through restructuring of information nodes. Knowledge is also constructed and not transmitted; therefore, meanings are used to construct appropriate links between concepts (Jonassen, et al., 2000). Furthermore, knowledge is the foundation for learning; it is the goal of the process.

There are three basic types of knowledge: declarative, procedural, and structural (Jonassen, et al., 1993). Structural knowledge is associated with long-term memory in that both focus on the storage of information. Structural knowledge mediates between declarative and procedural knowledge by providing organization and meaning to acquired knowledge. The process can be viewed as such: Declarative knowledge is awareness of an object, idea or concept, whereas procedural knowledge is the application of declarative knowledge into guidelines for performance. Structural knowledge is the organization of related nodes of information; it is how concepts are interrelated. It is through this organization and concept interrelatedness that action can be taken (procedural knowledge) based on awareness of a concept (declarative knowledge). Structural knowledge, more specifically than overall knowledge, is the actual basis for learning. Learning is defined as the building of new knowledge structures or the reorganization of existing knowledge structures (Jonassen, 1988, 1993; Jonassen, et al., 1993). Knowledge structure may also be referred to as cognitive structure or conceptual knowledge, but these appear to be terminology issues, as the basic concept remains the same (Jonassen, et al., 1993).

The final subprocess is retrieval and it entails searching through the associative links for specific information, which is activated once it is found (Lang, 2000). Pieces of information that have been more completely stored by connections through multiple links are more easily retrieved.

Also, as noted earlier, how information is originally encoded can help in its later retrieval, especially when retrieval cues are used (Tulving & Osler, 1968; Tulving & Patterson, 1968; Tulving & Thomson, 1973).

The process of learning outlined by the Limited Capacity Model highlights stages in which information is received, processed, and stored for later retrieval. We can make this process more efficient by focusing on the storage portion of the model. If concepts are linked in a meaningful way it should be easier to access particular pieces of information. Deep processing of information should help to create such meaningful linkages.

*Elaboration.* Elaboration has been defined as a method of adding learned information to knowledge by linking the new information to previously acquired information through examples, inferences, or other means (Schunk, 2000). The concept has been referred to by several different terms such as information processing (Weinstein, Zimmermann, & Palmer, 1988), covert cognitive processes (Kardash & Amlund, 1991), synthesis-analysis (Schmek, Ribich, & Ramanaiah, 1977), as well as deep or elaborative processing (Entwistle & Waterston, 1988; Schmek, 1983; Schmek, 1988; Schmek, Geisler-Brenstein, & Cercy, 1991). Although the terms differ in each of these articles, the concept remains very similar in each and generally focuses on an active attempt to process information by thinking deeply about it, connecting it to previously acquired information, or mentally applying it to situations.

Elaboration has been studied in relation to memory. Craik and Lockhart (1972) suggest that deeper processing in the form of elaboration is necessary to improve memory, or long term retention of information in memory. Furthermore, Seifert (1993) examined elaborative interrogation, a process in which individuals make inferences to newly acquired information by asking themselves *why* this information might be related to some other fact. He found that elaboration led to better memory for main concepts.

Examining elaboration during web use, Eveland and Dunwoody (2000) examined information processing while using a web site and found that

25% of the thoughts expressed by participants indicated elaborative thoughts concerning the information encountered. Elaboration also has been found to interact with motivation to predict knowledge structure density (KSD), (Eveland, Cortese, Park, & Dunwoody, 2004). In this particular instance, motivation was manipulated as either learning or browsing while using a web site. When browsing, elaboration was negatively related to KSD; however, when attempting to learn information elaboration was positively related to density.

Elaboration is considered to be important in improving memory (Craik & Lockhart, 1972). Research has backed up this claim (Seifert, 1993); however, findings are still tenuous when moving beyond simple recall and recognition and applying elaboration to knowledge structure (Eveland, Cortese, et al., 2004).

## Measuring Learning

There are three basic ways to measure learning: recall, recognition, and structural knowledge assessment. Recall can be measured using either cued or free recall. Cued recall utilizes prompts to assess recall of specific information, whereas free recall requires non-specific, non-cued information retrieval about a given topic. In an empirical examination of cued recall and recognition as learning outcomes, results indicated that the two methods of retrieval were equally effective as outcome assessments (Clariana & Lee, 2001).

*Structural Knowledge.* Jonassen, et al. (1993) proposed many ways of analyzing structural knowledge. They divided these methods into two overall categories, representing / assessing structural knowledge and conveying structural knowledge. The authors suggested that there are two ways to examine structural knowledge in terms of representation / assessment: Eliciting knowledge and representing structural knowledge. These concepts suggest that knowledge is first elicited by accessing stored knowledge, and then the underlying structure for that knowledge can be represented. The methods for eliciting and representing knowledge are all based on spatial issues related to the semantic proximities between concepts. Such techniques include word association proximities, similarity ratings, card sort, and tree construction tasks. The basis for each of these techniques is the perceived proximity of the concepts in the knowledge structure. Concepts that are closer together should be activated more quickly than those that are further apart. Conveying structural knowledge is associated with more demanding tasks that require higher-order mental operations. These techniques are more explicit and require the actual mapping of knowledge structure. Some suggested techniques include semantic maps, concept maps, spider maps, and graphic organizers (see Jonassen, et al., 1993 for further information regarding these techniques). The important distinction to keep in mind is that there are detailed techniques for assessing structure and organization and less detailed techniques that tap structure and organization without explicitly analyzing them.

Knowledge density has been helpful in understanding knowledge structure. Density has been applied to hypermedia systems as a way of examining the connectedness of the informational nodes comprising the system (Astleitner & Leutner, 1996). It is calculated by counting the number of links in the system and then dividing this number by the sum of all possible links. Researchers have also applied density to human knowledge structures as a measure of node connectedness (Eveland, Cortese, et al., 2004; Eveland, Marton, & Seo, 2004). The format for this analysis requires that the subject create a matrix of concepts (concepts can either be freely recalled by the subject or provided by the researcher) by listing all concepts on the top and left of the matrix. Then, they can indicate relatedness of each concept to every other concept in the space where each intersects in the matrix. A density score can then be calculated.

One technique for analyzing knowledge structure is concept mapping. According to Jonassen, et al. (1993), in comparison with other techniques for representing knowledge structure, concept mapping is the most appropriate. Concept mapping is a graphical representation of relationships between concepts using words to indicate the semantic relationship between concepts (Novak & Gowin, 1984). Therefore, concept mapping not only indicates that concepts are linked together; it stipulates the nature of the relationship. Concept maps are useful tools in examining what a learner knows by representing his / her knowledge structure. However, as Novak and Gowin noted, they do not suggest that concept mapping will result in a complete representation of this knowledge structure. Furthermore, they recommended that students be trained in this technique so that they acquire skills for concept mapping. They further suggested that concept maps must be redrawn, as the first concept map an individual draws will most definitely have errors. These final comments should serve as cautionary notes to researchers intending to use concept maps as representations of knowledge structure. Although a valuable tool, researchers must consider the facts that the concept maps provided by subjects may not be complete representations of knowledge structure, may contain errors, and will improve as the subjects' concept mapping skills improve. Research has indicated that the concept maps of experts more closely match actual subject concept connections than cognitive maps of students (Jonassen, et al., 1993). In addition to using concept maps as tools for assessing knowledge structure, concept maps can also be valuable in helping students to learn information by having them focus on relationships between concepts (Novak, 1990; Novak & Gowin, 1984).

Pathfinder networks are similar to concept mapping, but allow for easier comparison between human knowledge structures and information structures presented on a website. Pathfinder networks provide a technique to analyze connections between nodes by examining the link structure between those nodes. Links between concepts can be direct or indirect such that two concepts can be directly connected without the aid of a mediating concept or they can be linked indirectly through a third concept (Jonassen, et al., 1993). Furthermore, pathfinder networks analyze proximity data using algorithms that express the nodal connection structure and eliminate all paths but the most frequently occurring path (as indicated by the proximity data). The final result is a series of connections that portrays the most frequently chosen paths between each pair of nodes in the system (Barab, Fajen, Kulikowich, & Young, 1996). Pathfinder networks can be applied to both human knowledge structures and web-based information structures, allowing the two to be compared for similarities. Furthermore, because the pathfinder networks are generated from proximity data, it does not require individuals to actually generate concept maps. The data needed for such an analysis can be garnered from a matrix of concepts (similar to that described above in the discussion of density) using values to indicate the strength of each relationship instead of merely indicating a dichotomous (yes / no) relationship between each concept. For instance, subjects could be asked to indicate the strength of each relationship using a 1 (*weakly related*) to 7 (*strongly related*) scale (Jonassen, et al.). It should be noted that computer based programs can automate the process of generating pathfinder networks based on the proximity data provided (Jonassen, et al., 1993).

*Environment / Hypermedia*

The purpose of this study was to examine hypermedia learning from the WWW. The focus was not on web-enhanced courses, but use of the WWW as an information provider. Furthermore, the focus of this study was on the web of interconnected pages of information known as the WWW and not the more broadly based Internet, which encompasses not only this web of pages, but also e-mail and other devices for interpersonal communication between individuals.

Often the terms hypermedia and hypertext are used interchangeably. Generally, this is not a problem because the two concepts are quite similar. Hypertext can be defined as pieces of linked information or as a web of linked information (Bieber, 2000). Hypermedia has also been defined as a network of linked nodes of information (Bieber, Vitali, Ashman, Balasubramanian, & Oinas-Kukkonen, 1997). The underlying element that makes both of these terms hyper-*technologies* is that they structure information nonlinearly by connecting nodes of information. The distinction is that hypertext utilizes information in the form of text, whereas hypermedia utilizes information that can be derived from other media elements such as video, audio, and graphical representations (Bieber, 2000). Therefore, for the remainder of this text, the term hypermedia will be used, but with the assumption that this term actually encompasses both hypermedia and hypertext.

As indicated by the definitions above, the defining characteristic of hypermedia is that it presents information in a nonlinear format. Referencing the earlier work of Ted Nelson, Horney (1993) defined nonlinearity as a structure of information where users can follow personally defined paths of navigation. Hypermedia is simply a format for presentation in which the user or audience member has the ability to examine the content in a nonlinear fashion. What distinguishes hypermedia from multimedia is that it contains depth and richness in the information presented and allows the user to choose how much depth and richness to use (Jonassen & Mandl, 1989).

Hypermedia Characteristics

Hypermedia possesses key characteristics that make it useful when applied to learning (Jonassen, 1988). One characteristic is that hypermedia provides the learner with immediate and constant access to large quantities of information. A second characteristic is that hypermedia allows learners to structure information as they wish without being constrained by the author's organization structure. Third, through its use of a nonlinear structure, hypermedia allows designers to link together pieces of information in such a way as to make those relationships obvious to the learner. Fourth, hypermedia and the human brain share the same underlying structure, that of nodes of information that are interconnected through associative links. The third and fourth characteristics particularly add understanding to the study of the WWW as a learning environment and require further discussion.

The nonlinear structure of hypermedia allows the author to link together pieces of information in a way that should help the learner make connections. However, research has indicated that outcomes based on hypermedia use differ in terms of information seeking and learning.

For instance, researchers have encountered mixed results when studying the effects of nonlinearity on locating and learning information. McDonald and Stevenson (1996) compared three versions of hypermedia information presentation: A linear version using "back" and "next" buttons, a hierarchical version in which node connections specified a hierarchy of information, and a nonlinear version in which all nodes were connected to one another. Dependent variables for this study consisted of a series of tasks requiring participants to read and locate information, answer questions, and report on their experience using the system. Participants in the linear group outperformed those in the other two groups on all tasks except in their accuracy in answering questions. Participants also performed better using the hierarchical structure than when using the nonlinear structure, indicating that individuals performed better when more constraints were placed upon them. McDonald and Stevenson (1998a) conducted a similar study, this time using the hierarchy and nonlinear designs, but replacing the linear condition with a mixed condition. The mixed condition combined elements from the hierarchy and nonlinear condition in that it utilized the hierarchy structure in which nodes were connected to specified topics, but some of the nodes in the hierarchy were also connected across levels. Dependent variables for this study included browsing measures and navigation measures as indicators of ease of hypermedia use. Results indicated that those in the mixed condition displayed the most ease in using hypermedia systems.

Research in this area has also revealed different results depending on the type of learning outcome examined. For instance, research has indicated that nonlinear designs hinder factual learning and free recall, but they may help learners to see connections between pieces of information (as measured by knowledge density; Eveland, Cortese, et al., 2004; Eveland, Marton, et al., 2004; see also Eveland, Seo, & Marton, 2002); and recognition of information is higher when learning from a linear print presentation than when learning from both linear and nonlinear web presentations (Eveland & Dunwoody, 2001). Also, in a comparison of print versus online news, readers of an online version of the *New York Times* were less likely to recall and recognize information they encountered than those exposed to the print version of the newspaper (Tewksbury & Althaus, 2000).

Prior knowledge is often considered in this examination between non-linearity and learning. For instance, in one experiment, although knowledgeable and non-knowledgeable subjects did not differ in their browsing behavior using three different hypermedia formats (linear, nonlinear, and mixed), they did differ in their reading comprehension. Knowledgeable participants achieved higher reading comprehension scores than non-knowledgeable participants using the linear format. Also, non-knowledgeable participants achieved higher reading comprehension scores in the mixed condition than in the linear condition (Calisir & Gurel, 2003). This finding may add support to previous research indicating that non-knowledgeable hypermedia users rely more on navigational aids (such as a map of the hypermedia structure) than knowledgeable users when seeking and retrieving information (McDonald & Stevenson, 1998b). In another study, researchers used a pre / post-knowledge measure and found that participants with low prior subject knowledge increased their overall comprehension of the subject matter when using a hierarchical format (Potelle & Rouet 2003). However, these findings were not replicated in the networked and alphabetical list formats that were also examined. Also, this increase in comprehension only occurred at the global level. Participants did not experience an increase in comprehension when asked about specifically stated information within the text (local level). High prior subject knowledge participants did not experience any changes in their comprehension across the three conditions.

The examination of linearity within hypertext is not an element in the current study; however, a basic understanding of the type of research that exists in this area is valuable to consider because it is a characteristic of hypermedia. Furthermore, it is closely connected to the next characteristic of hypermedia.

The fourth characteristic of hypermedia, that it shares the same underlying structure with the human brain, suggests that hypermedia should play a major role in the learning process. Two theories of knowledge structure that specify this assumption are schema theory and spreading activation theory (Jonassen, et al., 1993). Schemas are nodes of stored information that represent our constructs for ideas, objects, and events. Schemas are related and connected to other schema, which gives them meaning. These connections form semantic networks of schema (called schemata). Spreading activation theory takes this notion a step further by suggesting that when we encounter a new piece of information, it activates a node in our knowledge structure. This activation spreads through to all the nodes connected to the originally activated node.

Hypermedia and Learning Theories

Researchers have applied behaviorist, cognitivist, and constructivist theories to hypermedia learning. When focusing on this connection, many researchers suggest ways in which instructional design can be enhanced by considering elements of each perspective. For instance, Ertmer and Newby (1993) suggested that because these three classes of theories can be considered a continuum of learning principles, instruction focus shifts from teaching to learning and from passive information presentation to active application of information. Behaviorism is grounded as a stimulus / response model; therefore, instructional design that utilizes prompts designed to evoke a particular response would align most with the assumptions of this perspective. Cognitivism can be elicited in instructional design by focusing on the organization of material (such as using outlines and summaries) and the presentation of analogies and examples to aid in comprehension. This can be achieved through practice sessions with feedback. Constructivism can be used by focusing student attention on meaning making as it relates to the context in which learning occurs, as well as placing the learner in control of the environment by presenting information in a variety of ways so that the learner can manipulate it. The inherent design of hypermedia material implies structure and meaning through associative hypermedia links. Furthermore, hypermedia use can actively engage students by providing them with control over their learning environment.

Kettanurak, Ramamuthy, and Haseman (2001) suggested more specific design techniques by focusing their analysis on interactive multimedia instruction (IMI). IMI utilizes multimedia components to deliver interactive classroom-like instruction via the Internet. It can be considered a form of hypermedia, therefore the theories and design concepts described here can be applied to both hypermedia and IMI systems that are designed solely for instructional purposes. Behaviorist theory focuses on the actions taken by learners and the notion of reinforcing positive behaviors that lead to learning. Hypermedia design features that can enforce behaviorist learning include feedback from the system and elements of learner control. Learner control is a concept based on the belief that the learner is in control of his / her learning environment. It places emphasis on active learners, willing to take control of their environment (Gabbard, 2000). Although Kettanurak, et al. (2001) place learner control under behaviorist theory, it has also been argued that learner control applies to tenets of both cognitivist and constructivist theories as well (Ertmer & Newby, 1993). The use of feedback (in the form of verification and error reports, and summary statistics of learning progress) and allowing learners to take control of their environment by setting their own pace and sequence of information exposure can help to reinforce positive learning behaviors.

Cognitivist theory focuses on what learners know and how they know it. It is concerned with the cognitive processes learners engage in while learning. Design principles that relate to cognitivist theory include techniques for eliciting and maintaining user attention, promoting positive attitudes toward content to keep learners motivated, and issues related to encoding, storage, and retrieval of information (Ertmer & Newby, 1993). Specific elements that incorporate cognitivist ideas include question asking (hot spots linked to further information), practice using and applying information, examples, and clear navigation structure. Finally, Kettanurak, et al. (2001) defined constructivist theory as focusing on learning as a process in which learners are taught to think and learn productively through the use of personal experience, situated cognition, and learning based on discovery. Design features include flexibility and active participation by the learners. They suggest that the inherent design of hypermedia lends itself to this theory through its nonlinear structure.

***Constructivism.*** Of these three theories, constructivism has received a great deal of attention from researchers in applying hypermedia to learning. A key component in constructivism is meaning making. In order to achieve meaningful learning, the learner must demonstrate intentionality, activity, and reflection (Jonassen, et al., 2000). Constructivist learning often begins with a question or dissonance encountered by the learner. The learner then embarks on an intentional and active search to solve the question or relieve the dissonance they encountered. It is through this search for information and reflection on that information that meaning is constructed and applied to the situation under investigation. Hypermedia is viewed as a tool for constructivist learning; it helps learners to construct and reconstruct meaning. Jonassen, et al. (2000) used intentional information seeking as an example of constructivist learning as it applies to hypermedia. When an individual engages in intentional information seeking on the WWW to resolve an informational need, elements of the WWW allow users to specify their intentions through searches and focus attention on tasks by providing information specific to the current informational need. As the learner is presented with information, s/he must constantly reflect on that information and construct meaning. It is important to note that meaning making is specific to the individual and that, although message creators have a particular meaning in mind that they wish to impart, not everyone will interpret that message in the same way (Jonassen, et al., 2000; Gabbard, 2000).

Hypermedia and Learning

Research has provided mixed results when examining the link between hypermedia and learning. The following issues are addressed as they relate to hypermedia learning: use, factual knowledge, structural knowledge, and elaboration enhanced web design.

*Hypermedia Use.* Hypermedia users tend to follow the suggested structure of a given website. For instance, when presented with a graphical representation of a site's link structure, users will navigate through a website based on this suggested structure (de Jong & van der Hulst, 2002). Even when more subtle structure cues are presented (such as random placement of nodes that are highlighted to suggest a hierarchy), individuals still tend to follow the structure that is represented. In a sense, users tend to navigate linearly through a website, even though nonlinear navigation is possible. Eveland and Dunwoody (1998) noted that when presented with a list of links, subjects chose the first link 75% of the time. Once in the site, users tend to use in-text links over back / next buttons provided at the bottom of a hypermedia page.

Often experiments assessing hypermedia use for information gain will examine how people search for particular pieces of information and whether or not that searching aids learning. This is determined when examining the efficiency with which individuals search through information. Nilsson and Mayer (2002) concluded that individuals did not integrate information covered when using a site with a graphical map browser. They concluded that subjects did not need to engage in such processing because the map was always available to them. Therefore, their searches did not become more efficient in terms of number of links visited. Search tasks were found to be more efficient (measured by number of repeat links visited) when using a mixed condition website in which a hierarchical organization was combined with nonlinear links thereby creating a site that is not wholly hierarchical or nonlinear (McDonald & Stevenson, 1998a). Specifically, such a site includes a basic hierarchy of concepts that are linked as a hierarchy with nonlinear links leading to information that violates the hierarchy structure by connecting across and between various levels. In a similar study, efficient searching occurred most frequently when using a graphical map as a navigational aid as opposed to a list of topics as a navigational aid (ranked second in efficiency) and a hyptertext with no navigational aids (McDonald & Stevenson, 1998b). However, when comparing linear and nonlinear structures, subjects performed better using a linear site in terms of speed and accuracy in accomplishing the search task (McDonald & Stevenson, 1996).

Moving beyond the basic search task, Cress and Knabel (2003) found that when comparing browsing versus search conditions, those in the browsing condition acquired more knowledge gain. In this particular study, those in the browse condition were asked to understand as much of the content as possible and those in the search task were asked to find words missing from sentences. In addition to learning more in the browse condition, these subjects also evaluated the site more positively than those in the search condition.

***Factual and Structural Knowledge.*** Learning results can differ based on the form of information presentation. When specifically applied to hypermedia learning, researchers have found that different learning results can be found when different knowledge measures are used (de Jong & van der Hulst, 2002) and different hypermedia structures influence different types of learning (Eveland, Cortese, et al., 2004).

When comparing online sources to other forms of media, online media appear to obstruct recall and recognition but enhance knowledge structure. Using the same information stimulus, individuals who examined the print version displayed greater recognition (Eveland & Dunwoody, 2001) and recall (Lee & Tedder, 2003) than those viewing the nonlinear online version. Also, when focusing on recall, both print and TV news use resulted in higher recall than an online version of the news (Eveland, et al., 2002). However, the online display resulted in greater KSD (measured using Adjusted Ratio of Clustering) than TV and print news.

Results have also varied depending on the form of online presentation. Linear presentations have indicated better factual knowledge than nonlinear presentations, but use of nonlinear presentations has resulted in better KSD when compared to linear presentations (Eveland, Cortese, et al., 2004; Eveland, Marton, et al., 2004).

Jonassen used a HyperCard version of a printed hypermedia system to analyze the relationship between hypermedia and structural knowledge (Jonassen, 1993; Jonassen & Wang, 1993). Three studies were employed, each examining the same dependent variables: recall and structural knowledge. The researchers developed specific measures to examine structural knowledge that focused on relationship proximity, semantic relationships, and analogies between concepts.

The first study examined differences based on three forms of presentation: list, map, and link window (See Jonassen, 1993; Jonassen & Wang, 1993). The map presentation utilized a graphical browser that linked to all nodes. The graphical browser depicted the structure of connections between concepts. The link window presentation also linked to all nodes, but the presentation was simply a list of terms instead of the graphical map of related concepts. When users scrolled over listed items, a pop-up window was displayed describing the nature of the relationship between concepts. The list presentation served as a control condition and provided no structural information to the user. Results from this study indicated that structural knowledge scores were the same for all three groups, but recall scores were higher for the control (list only) group.

In the second study the researchers manipulated generative learning, in which learners relate new information to previously acquired information in personally meaningful ways (See Jonassen, 1993; Jonassen & Wang, 1993). This study used the link window and list treatments from the first study. In order to examine generative learning, the third condition presented subjects with a similar display as the link window, except explicit relationships were not detailed. Instead, subjects were asked to generate the nature of each link themselves. Results from this study echoed that of study one in that the control group performed better on the recall task, but there were no differences among groups on the structural knowledge assessments.

The focus of the third study was on semantic networks (See Jonassen, 1993; Jonassen & Wang, 1993). The two treatment groups in this study were the same as the list and map groups from study one. A second manipulation was used in that half the subjects were instructed to create semantic networks of the content using a semantic network program. The remaining subjects were not asked to complete this task. Results from this study indicated that the group using the semantic network task achieved higher scores on the structural knowledge assessments than those who did not create semantic networks.

The researchers pointed out that some important conclusions emerged from these studies (Jonassen, 1993; Jonassen & Wang, 1993). First, the presence of structural cues in hypermedia will not automatically result in increases in structural knowledge acquisition. Structural cues may even be distracting and hinder simple recall tasks as well. Second, simple browsing of hypermedia does not engage the learner enough to support meaningful learning. Third, experienced hypermedia users should be the focus of such studies in order to actually test their ability to gain and integrate information acquired through hypermedia. Experienced users will have developed strategies for navigating through hypermedia and could provide further insight into this issue. Fourth, results from these studies make it questionable as to whether or not meaningful learning can result from hypermedia use. The benefit of hypermedia may be in its ability to serve as an information retrieval tool.

In another study, de Jong and van der Hulst (2002) also examined various forms of learning by manipulating site structure. The three stimulus conditions included a *visual* condition in which a graphical hierarchy of the site was presented as a navigational tool, a *hints* condition in which graphical nodes were randomly ordered but highlighted to suggest the hierarchy that was detailed in the visual condition, and a *control* condition in which the graphical nodes were randomly presented, but not highlighted. Subjects were presented with pre- and posttest knowledge measures in the form of definitional knowledge (multiple choice regarding the definitions of concepts), propositional knowledge (multiple choice assessing the relationship between concepts) and configural knowledge (assessed using a card sort technique). Results indicated that those in the visual condition had higher gains in propositional and configural knowledge than those in the control condition, but there was no difference in definitional knowledge across conditions. These results are clearly contradictory to those found by Jonassen (1993), Jonassen and Wang (1993). In response, de Jong and van der Hulst suggested that it is due to the fact that different knowledge measures result in different learning outcomes. However, as noted earlier, more recent research has indicated a connection between nonlinear site design and greater KSD (Eveland, Cortese, et al., 2004; Eveland, Marton, et al., 2004).

The one aspect of the earlier Jonassen studies that was utilized by de Jong and van der Hulst (2002) was that they employed graphical browsers in their study. In another study, a different aspect of the Jonassen studies was adapted for examination—the link window.

Cress and Knabel (2003) used pop-up windows activated by clicking in-text links. These pop-up windows summarized information to be found on the page associated with each particular link. This manipulation differs from Jonassen's work (Jonassen, 1993; Jonassen & Wang, 1993) in that Jonassen specified the relationships between the current item and the linked item and Cress and Knabel merely provided the summary of the linked item. They used two manipulations in their study, the preview / no preview manipulation and a search / browse task manipulation. Search task results were evaluated in terms of the number of correct answers reported for the search item questions and knowledge gain was assessed by comparing answers to pre and post multiple-choice knowledge tests. Log files indicated that previews decreased the number of pages accessed thereby reducing the amount of information reviewed. Previews had no effect on the search task, however, for the browse task, those in the preview condition displayed more knowledge gain than those in the no preview condition.

***Elaboration and Web Design.*** Deep processing in the form of elaboration is considered important to improve memory (Craik & Lockhart, 1972). Elaborative interrogations in which individuals actively process why pieces of information are related has led to better memory for main concepts (Seifert, 1993). Furthermore, using a think aloud technique and a science information website, results from one study indicated that 25% of thoughts expressed by participants were elaborative in nature (Eveland & Dunwoody, 2000). However, when elaboration has been used as a manipulation in web information knowledge studies, no effects have emerged (Eveland, Cortese, et al., 2004; Eveland, Marton, et al., 2004). It would appear that even though individuals are encouraged to elaborate content on a website, they may not actually be doing so, or do so without encouragement.

Many of the studies discussed to this point have manipulated site design, which may be the key to understanding these issues further. When asked to actually design a site, subjects displayed a high degree of engagement in the task of organizing information and when comparing pre- and post-knowledge structure measure, the average number of chunks of information increased after the task (Chen & McGrath, 2003). In looking at use of a predesigned site, Tremayne and Dunwoody (2001) found that a complex site (utilizing more user options than the less complex site) was associated with more elaboration, more interactive behavior (mouse and keyboard activity) and greater recall.

Hypertext links are a main consideration in hypermedia design. The function of hypertext links is to order reading for the user, bridge gaps between pieces of information, and provide the user with cues enabling them to sense a shift in focus as they move from one concept to another (Morgan, 2002). Learners need to make meaningful connections between links both as designers and as users. Furthermore, tools such as navigation aids and online help could lessen cognitive burden and enhance learning (Leung, 2003).

Clearly there are still some unanswered questions in this area. For instance, if nonlinear designs do indeed advance knowledge structure, why do they hinder factual knowledge (Eveland, Cortese, et al., 2004; Eveland, Marton, et al., 2004)? Also, it appears that pop-up windows that display summary information may aid factual knowledge (Cress & Knabel, 2003), but pop-ups using relational information do not seem to aid knowledge structure (Jonassen, 1993; Jonassen & Wang, 1993). In-text links alone should encourage users to elaborate connections between concepts, but this may not always be the case. A form of elaboration manipulation can be built into a website using pop-up windows similar to those used in previous studies. However, within these pop-up windows the participants are asked to think about the information contained in these pop-up windows. That is, the definitional pop-up window asks participants to think about the displayed definition of the hyperlinked word (as opposed to a summary of information on the page being accessed) by comparing it to previously acquired knowledge and experiences. This should lead to definitional knowledge acquisitions (a form of recognition related to identifying term definitions). Similarly, a relational elaboration pop-up window asks participants to think about the displayed description of the relationship between the current concept and the hyperlinked concept by connecting this information to previously acquired knowledge or experiences. This form of elaboration manipulation should promote KSD. It is important to match the type of learning assessed with the type of elaboration used because different learning results can be found based on the types of measures used (de Jong & van der Hulst, 2002). If this technique is used, the question then becomes, can website structure (and content) be manipulated in order to enhance learning? With this question in mind, the following hypotheses were posed:

*H1a:   A definitional elaboration website design will foster greater definitional knowledge when compared to a relational elaboration website design and a basic nonlinear website design.*

*H1b:   A relational elaboration website design will foster greater knowledge structure density when compared to a definitional elaboration website design and a basic nonlinear website design.*

Research findings regarding factual knowledge in the realm of hypermedia information has suggested that nonlinear presentations hinder factual knowledge gain (Eveland, Cortese, et al., 2004; Eveland, Marton, et al., 2004). However, it is not clear how the use of relational and definitional elaboration sites may impact this relationship; therefore, the following research question was posed:

> *RQ1:   When comparing three websites (basic nonlinear, definitional elaboration, and relational elaboration), which will foster more factual knowledge?*

## Personal Factors / Human Agency

Personal factors are individual characteristics that influence and are influenced by behaviors and the environment. Various personal factors emerge when hypermedia formats are used for learning.

### Subject Expertise

Past research provides insight into the connections between user subject expertise and online learning by suggesting that experienced users navigate hypermedia more efficiently. For instance, students with greater subject knowledge show more purposeful web navigation by allocating their time to various nodes of information in a more purposive and selective manner than those with less subject knowledge (MacGregor, 1999). Knowledgeable users also spend less time visiting the same links repeatedly (McDonald & Stevenson, 1998a) and rely less on navigational aids (McDonald & Stevenson, 1998b) than less knowledgeable users. Experts browse fewer topics and in more depth, rely less on referential links, examine topics that appear to be based on expertise, browse topics appealing to special interests, and compare information to their own structural knowledge for evaluation (Carmel, Stephen, & Chen, 1992). Furthermore, individuals with prior subject knowledge tend to be more successful at a task than those without prior knowledge (Steinberg, 1989). With this in mind, subject expertise should enhance results associated with the task of learning from the Internet.

Based on this evidence, those with subject expertise should display higher knowledge than those without subject expertise. However, elaborative cues in the web structure may enhance learning for those with less expertise by helping them to navigate more efficiently. Therefore, the following hypotheses were posed:

> *H2a:   There will be an interaction between subject expertise and site design such that those low in sub-ject expertise will display higher definitional knowledge when using a definitional elaboration website than when using a basic nonlinear design; whereas those high in sub-ject expertise will display similar definitional knowledge in both the definitional and basic design conditions.*

> *H2b:   There will be an interaction between subject expertise and site design such that those low in sub-ject expertise will display higher knowledge structure density when using a relational elaboration website than when using a basic nonlinear design; whereas those high in subject expertise will display similar knowledge structure density in both the relational and basic design conditions.*

Past literature has not taken into account various forms of elaboration and how they may impact factual knowledge. Therefore, the following research question was tested:

> *RQ2:   Will subject expertise interact with the site design (basic nonlinear, definitional elaboration, and relational elaboration) to increase factual knowledge?*

## Web Expertise

When applying expertise to the activity of hypermedia browsing, more experienced hypertext users tend to search nonlinearly, whereas novices use hypertext more linearly (Qiu, 1993). An experiment of content presentation indicated that web experts learned more than novices when using both print and web delivered information (Eveland & Dunwoody, 2001). The authors attribute this finding to the fact that the web presents print information in an electronic form and that it is a supplement to and not a replacement for traditional forms of media. Unz and Hesse (1999) suggested that both learning and information skills should be considered because both are needed to navigate the web successfully. However, it is important to realize that in the context of information seeking, skilled web users are not necessarily better at gaining information than novice users. Skilled users are generally more efficient at locating information because, through repeated use, they become efficient at finding the information they need when they need it and not because they know a predetermined set of methods (based on predictions from a computationally-based performance model and not actual users; Howes & Payne, 1990). However, even skilled users can be expected to make errors (Kitajima & Polson, 1995).

Some general conclusions emerge from the previous discussion. Internet use expertise has been associated with greater learning (Eveland & Dunwoody, 2001). Skilled Internet users are expected to possess developed strategies for finding information, therefore making their searches more efficient (Howes & Payne, 1990). As with subject expertise, learners with low levels of web expertise may benefit from the use of elaboration embedded in the website structure. Therefore, the following hypotheses were examined:

> *H3a: There will be an interaction between web expertise and site design such that those low in web expertise will display higher definitional knowledge when using a definitional elaboration website than when using a basic nonlinear design; whereas those high in web expertise will display similar definitional knowledge in both the definitional and basic design conditions.*

*H3b: There will be an interaction between web expertise and site design such that those low in web expertise will display higher knowledge structure density when using a relational elaboration website than when using a basic nonlinear design; whereas those high in web expertise will display similar knowledge structure density in both the relational and basic design conditions.*

Again, past research does not lead to a clear hypothesis in the examination of factual knowledge as it relates to elaboration site manipulation. Therefore, just as with subject expertise, the following research question was tested regarding web expertise and factual knowledge across website conditions:

*RQ3: Will web expertise interact with site design (basic nonlinear, definitional elaboration, and relational elaboration) to increase factual knowledge?*

Motivation

Weiner (1992) defined motivation as the force that influences individuals to think and behave a certain way. Motivation is the underlying mechanism that energizes us to take action.

Drive theory (Hull, 1943) suggests that humans have needs that propel them to behave in certain ways. Later iterations of the theory (Hull, 1951) considered the importance of incentives, in that they add to our drive to engage in a behavior. Drive focuses attention on what pushes us to behave in a certain way. Drives can be interpreted as a push, whereas incentives pull an individual towards a desired goal (Weiner, 1992).

A mass media perspective that is closely connected to this focus on human needs as motivation for behavior is uses and gratifications (U&G). The U&G perspective has been widely used to examine motivations for media use. The perspective views media consumers as an active audience who are motivated to use particular media to satisfy certain needs or wants (Rubin, 1984). U&G researchers are concerned with antecedent variables that affect motives, as well as outcome variables that are affected by motives. This method of study comes from the basic objectives of the U&G paradigm, which are based on the idea that individuals are motivated by personal or societal attributes to use a medium. Also, after using the medium to satisfy a particular motive, personal or societal attributes may be affected (Katz, Blumler, & Gurevitch, 1974).

U&G has been widely applied to television use and more recently to Internet use. Researchers have identified a generally consistent list of motives for using most forms of media. Some of these motives including: relaxation, companionship, habit, pass time, entertainment, social interaction, information, arousal, and escape (Bantz, 1982; Ferguson & Perse, 2000; Papacharissi & Rubin, 2000; Rubin, 1983).

An inherent issue in the examination of motivation is the value of intrinsic versus extrinsic motivation. Intrinsic motivation is an internal motivation to succeed at a task because of personal interest or enjoyment, whereas extrinsic motivation is an instrumental motivation grounded in the consequences surrounding a task (Deci, Vallerand, Pelletier, & Ryan, 1991; Guay, Vallerand, & Blanchard, 2000; Vallerand & Ratelle, 2002). Specifically, extrinsic motivation can stem from the offer of incentives or to avoid negative consequences (external regulation), or as a way of achieving a desired outcome (identified regulation). In this last example, the task is not engaged in because of the task itself but because it is a means to a particular end. Using a meta-analysis of literature pertaining to motivation, Eisenberger and Cameron (1996) examined whether or not the use of rewards lessens interest in a task and creativity in performing the task. They concluded that, although there are negative effects of rewards on task interest and creativity, the negative effects are specific and limited to certain situations, and they can be resolved.

According to self-determinism theory (Deci & Ryan, 1985), learning can be enhanced by fostering an interest in learning and by elevating student confidence. Intrinsic motivation is a key factor in this theory because it requires students to look within for success. Students with self-determination were found to be more likely to stay in school, display achievement, show conceptual understanding, and be considered well adjusted than those with less self-determination (Deci, et al., 1991). Furthermore, when more extrinsic motivation is used (as with performance evaluations), students may feel the pressure of being controlled. Past research has indicated that the use of external motivation in a web-learning task actually led to less learning (Eveland & Dunwoody, 2001). As stipulated by Deci, et al., it is important for students to value learning. If they place value on their learning, they will be self-determined to focus on success.

This focus on success may be a mediating factor between motivation and learning. A motivation to learn may prompt an individual to devote more effort to the task by relying on various learning strategies they have used in the past (Palmer & Goetz, 1988). We develop our own ways of learning through trial and error with past learning experiences. Motivation can prompt a learner to expend more effort or commitment to learn information (Brown, 1988; Humphreys & Revelle, 1984). In doing so, they may utilize learning strategies that have proved helpful in the past. Although on-task effort and learning strategies may help to clarify the link between motivation and learning, they are beyond the scope of this study.

Intrinsic learning may be inherent in using the Internet to learn or find information. Generally, WWW users enter the online environment with an information need, therefore, they are already intrinsically motivated to locate information and learn the answer to their question. This is not to suggest that WWW users are always goal-oriented in their search tasks. As displayed by research using U&G, it is apparent that some users turn to the Internet not only for information, but to pass the time and to relax. However, it is assumed that most learners who engage the Internet for information acquisition will be intrinsically motivated to learn, and in doing so, they will devote the necessary effort to achieve their goal. Therefore, the following hypothesis was posed:

> *H4:   Intrinsic motivation will be positively related to definitional knowledge, knowledge structure density, and factual knowledge in all web design conditions.*

Self-efficacy

Self-efficacy is employed prior to engaging in a task and it is the perceived ability individuals possess for successful completion of a task (Bandura, 2001, 2002b). Metacognition, one's awareness of, and guidance over, one's activities (Royer, Cisero, & Carlo, 1993), is a main feature of human agency (Bandura, 2001). It is through this awareness that motivation and actions can be evaluated. Metacognition is a key element in self-efficacy in that awareness of our accomplishments can build or degenerate our future self-efficacy toward a similar task. When applied to learning, negative or limited metacognitions about learning abilities could lead to the use of defensive learning strategies (such as devaluating the learning experience; Brown, 1988) or the absence of learning strategies (Palmer & Goetz, 1988).

Self-efficacy is developed through four primary sources (Bandura, 1999). First, self-efficacy is developed through mastery experiences, which are personal experiences in which an individual achieves success at a task. Self-efficacy is increased through repeated success over difficult tasks. The second source is vicarious experience, which is when self-efficacy is increased due to the success of others. For instance, an individual's feeling that s/he can succeed at a task can be bolstered merely by witnessing another person succeed at the same task.The third source is social persuasion. Social persuasion occurs when an individual's self-efficacy is bolstered by others who convince him / her that s/he has the ability to succeed at a task. The fourth source is a reliance on physical and emotional states. How we feel physically and emotionally affects our sense of ability. Therefore, to increase efficacy, it is best to maintain positive physical and emotional well-being.

Research has indicated that self-efficacy enhances learning tasks. For instance, in an examination of self-efficacy in an online class, self-efficacy predicted final exam scores whereas study habits did not (Wang & Newlin, 2002). Self-efficacy in an Internet search task was found to have a positive relationship with the number of correct search responses reported (Thompson, Meriac, & Cope, 2002). Also, other factors such as age have been found to impact self-efficacy. In an examination using simple memory tasks to examine learning, researchers asked participants to recall shopping list items (West & Thorn, 2001). The experiment was conducted using two separate samples, an older group of subjects ($M = 70.7$ years of age) and a younger group ($M = 18.7$ years of age). Results indicated that younger adults tended to display higher self-efficacy and recall than older adults (West & Thorn, 2001).

The Hypertext Interaction Cycle (HIC) places emphasis on the importance of self-efficacy as it relates to motivation, goals, and feedback in the accomplishment of a computer mediated task (Fredin & David, 1998). The HIC can be applied to any type of human / computer interaction; however, it is quite useful in a browsing context where several websites are accessed. The cycle details user choices and behaviors at three stages: preparation (before browsing), exploration (during browsing), and consolidation. The consolidation phase occurs when exploration is exhausted and either pertinent information was found or searching of that particular web page is considered to be finished and a new page is accessed, at which time the cycle returns to the preparation stage. Self-efficacy changes and influences performance from cycle to cycle. Specifically, low global self-efficacy (confidence in achieving the overall task; occurs in the preparation phase) is linked to broad, unspecified goals in the first cycle. Because the goals are unspecified, success is likely to be high. Therefore, the user enters the next cycle with high local self-efficacy (confidence in achieving a particular task; occurs in the consolidation phase), which leads to high global self-efficacy in cycle two. This higher global self-efficacy leads to more confidence and more specified goals, which leaves open the potential for less success. If failure is encountered in cycle two, then the user enters cycle three with a lower local self-efficacy and, consequently, a lower global self-efficacy. Both self-efficacy and goals can change with success and failure in each cycle. An important implication of this research is that it stresses the need to examine self-efficacy as it relates to specific tasks and not just overall / global self-efficacy.

Self-efficacy helps us to feel confident in our abilities and to stay motivated to complete tasks. Past research has indicated the important role self-efficacy can play in the achievement of learning tasks (Wang & Newlin, 2002). Internet learning is the specific task of this study, so it is especially important to focus on Internet self-efficacy (ISE). Therefore, the following hypothesis was posed:

> *H5:   Self-efficacy will be positively related to definitional knowledge, knowledge structure density, and factual knowledge in all web design conditions.*

## Cognitive Load

Absorbing and understanding an abundance of information can be an overwhelming task for an individual. Cognitive Load Theory focuses on cognitive resource availability and allocation during learning and problem solving (Sweller, 1988; Sweller, Chandler, Tierney, & Cooper, 1990). Students must first master basic skills before moving on to more complex tasks because they do not have the cognitive resources available to concentrate on higher-order concepts (Sinclair, Renshaw, & Taylor, 2004). An examination of cognitive load comparing hypermedia versus print information revealed that hypermedia use led to higher perceived cognitive load and less comprehension of material (Macedo-Rouet, Rouet, Epstein, & Fayard, 2003). Larger levels of cognitive load were also found to relate to lower recognition scores after hypermedia use (Eveland & Dunwoody, 2001).

Additional information beyond what is normally encountered in a standard nonlinear design could add to the cognitive load of the hypermedia user by utilizing all available processing resources. Therefore, additional information incorporated into a web design may hinder learning because it requires users to attend to too much information. Thus, the following hypotheses were examined:

*H6a:    There will be an interaction between cognitive load and site design such that those who experience high cognitive load will display lower definitional knowledge when using a definitional elaboration website than when using a basic nonlinear design; whereas those low in cognitive load will display higher definitional knowledge when using a definitional elaboration website than when using a basic nonlinear design.*

*H6b:    There will be an interaction between cognitive load and site design such that those who experience high cognitive load will display lower knowledge structure density when using a relational elaboration website than when using a basic nonlinear design; whereas those low in cognitive load will display higher knowledge structure density when using a relational elaboration website than when using a basic nonlinear design.*

Because past research findings relating factual knowledge to nonlinear hypermedia content have been limited, it is difficult to hypothesize about the impact of cognitive load on this relationship. Therefore, the following research question was posed:

> *RQ6:   Will cognitive load interact with site design (basic nonlinear, definitional elaboration, relational elaboration) to decrease factual knowledge?*

## STUDY DESIGN

SCT provides a theoretical framework for the design of the proposed study. The three elements of the theory (personal factors, the environment, and behavior) suggest key variables for examination (see Figure 1). Personal factors such as subject expertise, web expertise, self-efficacy, motivation, and cognitive load can interact with the environment and impact learning. Therefore, these variables were included in the study (see Figure 2 for a study model). The WWW served as the environment for this study. Hypermedia has many characteristics that should lend itself to successful learning. A hypermedia environment was designed that focused on alternative medicine. This environment possesses a hierarchical structure of information with links to interconnected nodes of information. Furthermore, three versions of the environment were designed, two of which manipulate elaboration through the use of pop-up windows activated when using in-text links. Finally, the behavior of interest in this study was learning. Learning is viewed as a process from encoding to storage to retrieval. Learning was evaluated using cued recall and knowledge structure assessments utilizing concept relatedness data.

FIGURE 2.    Study Design Model

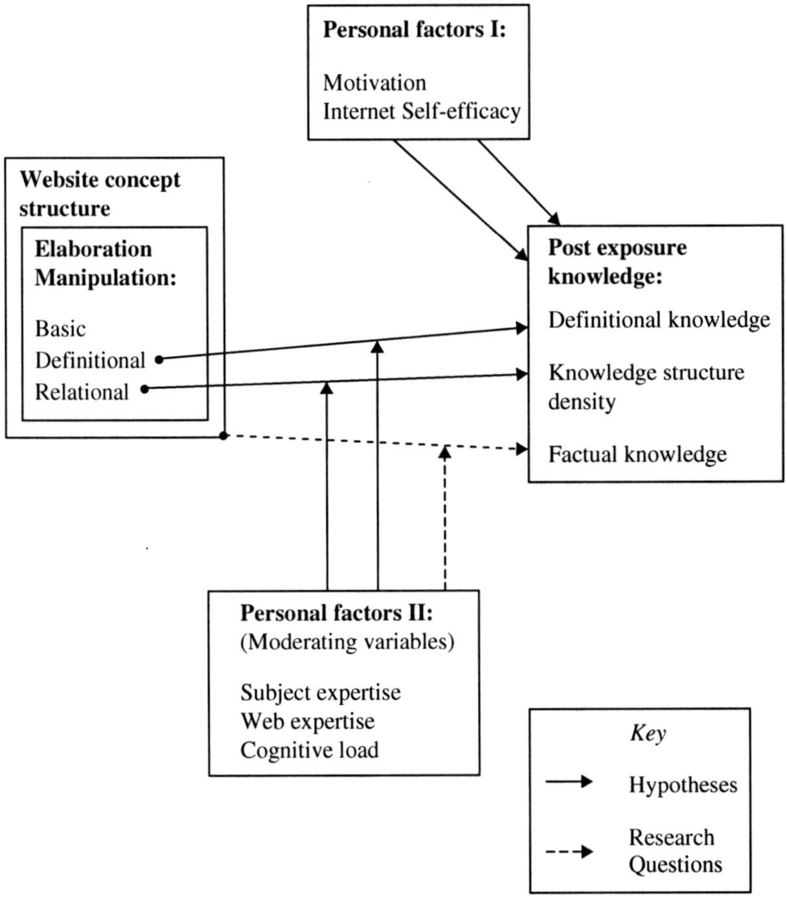

**Personal factors I:**

Motivation
Internet Self-efficacy

**Website concept structure**

**Elaboration Manipulation:**

Basic
Definitional
Relational

**Post exposure knowledge:**

Definitional knowledge

Knowledge structure density

Factual knowledge

**Personal factors II:**
(Moderating variables)

Subject expertise
Web expertise
Cognitive load

*Key*

⟶    Hypotheses

--→    Research Questions

CHAPTER TWO

# METHOD

The study design is further detailed in this chapter with a discussion of the experimental method used in this study. Specifically, this section focuses on issues related to the procedures, stimulus, sample, and measures used in conducting the experiment.

## PROCEDURE

The design for this study consisted of a control condition and two experimental conditions in which website design was manipulated. Three versions of the stimulus material were created: a basic nonlinear site (control), a definitional elaboration site, and a relational elaboration site. Two versions manipulated forms of elaboration using pop-up windows associated with hypertext links. Data was collected using responses to questionnaire items.

Participants were randomly assigned to one of three groups upon arrival at the testing area. The entire study was accessible online. Participants were first asked to indicate acceptance of the consent form. Next, they received a pretest containing questions that pertained to subject expertise, web expertise, Internet self-efficacy, and demographic information. Participants were then given instructions asking them to examine the website for approximately 20 minutes. They were asked to actively read through the content to understand the material, and, although a quiz would follow exposure, they were told not to try to memorize the content (see Appendix B for full instructions). After exposure to the stimulus website, participants answered a posttest questionnaire consisting of measures of motivation, cognitive load, elaboration manipulation checks, and learning (factual knowledge, definitional knowledge, and structural knowledge).

## STIMULUS

A website containing health information focusing on alternative medicine and techniques (i.e., acupuncture, acupressure, herbs, massage, yoga, meditation, detoxification, etc.) served as the stimulus material for this study. The site had a left-hand navigation bar and in-text links connecting pages of information. The site contained 27 pages: a basic introductory page to the site, six secondary homepages serving as subheading introductory pages, and 20 topic pages (See Figure 3). Each of the secondary homepages were accessible via a top horizontal navigation bar. Once on a secondary homepage, the topics associated with each particular page were contained on a left-hand navigation bar. In-text links also connected topics across information subgroups. Content for the site was drawn from existing websites and books about alternative medicine.

FIGURE 3. Stimulus Webpage Topic Structure

| Main Welcome Page (Homepage) | | | | | |
|---|---|---|---|---|---|
| Alternative Drug Therapy | Nutrition | Detoxification | Bodywork Techniques | Relaxation | Exercise |
| Herbal Remedies | Vegetarian | Fasting | Acupuncture | Aromatherapy | Yoga |
| Homeopathy | Raw Foods | Weekend Monodiets | Acupressure | Meditation | Tai Chi |
| Vitamins | Macrobiotics | Colon Therapies | Massage | QiGong | |
| | | Chelation Therapy | Reflexology | | |
| | | | Chiropractic | | |

The black row indicates the main / welcome page, grey indicates the secondary home pages, and white indicates topic pages within each general content area.

Three versions of this website were created in order to develop the elaboration design manipulation. The control condition, *basic*, consisted of the basic, nonlinear design described above (see Figure 4). The *definitional* condition was similar to the basic condition except that pop-up windows were connected to each in-text and left-hand navigation link. These pop-up windows defined the highlighted link term (this term corresponded to the connected page of information; see Figure 5). The *relational* condition also contained pop-up windows but the information displayed specified the relationship between the current node of information and the linked node of information (see Figure 6). All pop-ups were small windows that opened over the existing webpage. They had a "Click Here To Continue" link under the definition or relational information so that participants could move on to the selected node once they had sufficient time to read the information in the pop-up screen.

FIGURE 4.   Sample Page, Basic Site

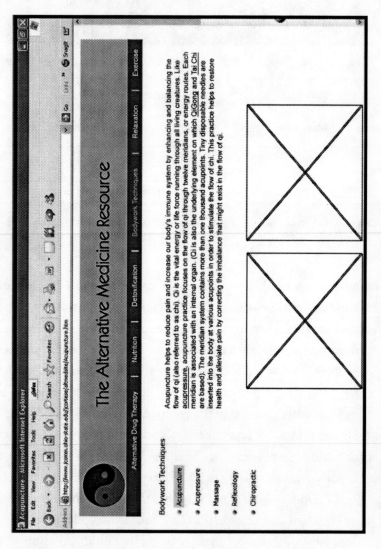

Actual website images have been removed and replaced with image placeholders.

FIGURE 5.    Sample Page, Definitional Site

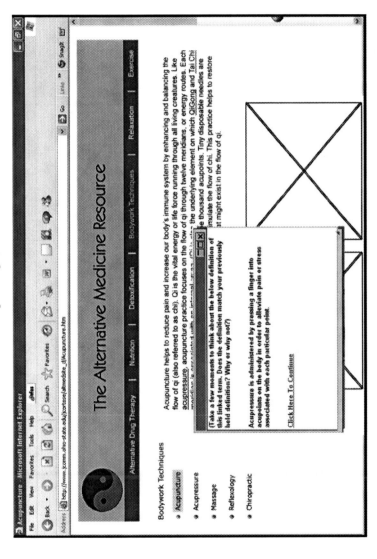

Actual website images have been removed and replaced with image placeholders.

FIGURE 6. Sample Page, Relational Site

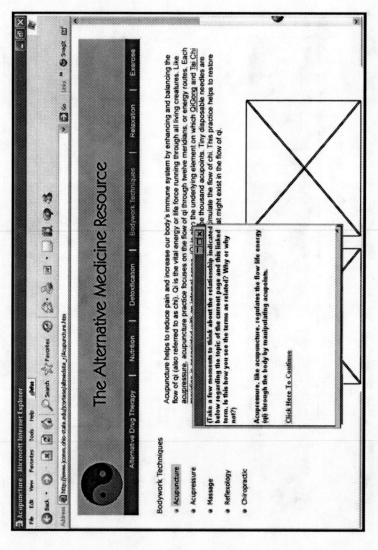

Actual website images have been removed and replaced with image placeholders.

## SAMPLE

The sample for the study consisted of undergraduate students from a large Midwestern university. Participants were recruited from communication courses and they were offered extra course credit for their participation. GPower (Faul & Erdfelder, 1992) analysis was used to determine a potential sample size for this study. Based on the effect size from a past, similar study (de Jong & van der Hulst, 2002) a sample size of 99 was needed. This number was calculated using an effect size of .3174, an alpha of .05, and a recommended power of .80 (Cohen, 1965). The actual sample size for this study was 156 participants. Details of this particular sample consist of age, gender, race, class rank, marital status, and income.

### Age

Participants were asked to indicate their age as of their last birthday. Ages ranged from 17 to 53 years, with an average age of 20.81 years ($SD = 3.34$).

### Gender

The gender composition of the sample for this study was 60.3% female ($N = 94$) and 39.7% male ($N = 62$).

### Race

Participants were asked to indicate, "the race you consider yourself" by choosing all options that apply. The majority of the sample indicated that they consider themselves to be Caucasian / White (85.9%, $N = 134$). Also, 9% considered themselves to be African-American ($N = 14$), 4.5% indicated Asian-American ($N = 7$), and 1.3% indicated that they were Hispanic ($N = 2$). Three participants (1.9%) indicated their race as "Other". One of the participants left the open-ended portion that accompanied the "Other" category blank, while another indicated that they were Native-American and the last indicated their race as "multi-racial."

## Class Rank

Participants were asked to indicate their current class standing. The majority of the sample consisted of upper-classmen, in that 30.8% were seniors ($N = 48$) and 29.5% were juniors ($N = 46$), whereas 22.4% were sophomores ($N = 35$) and 17.3% were freshmen ($N = 27$).

## Marital Status

In indicating their marital status, the vast majority of the sample reported being single (97.4%, $N = 152$). Three participants reported being married (1.9%) and one was divorced (.6%).

## Income

Participants were asked to provide their "estimated family income." The modal income reported by this sample was $70,000–$80,000. The majority of the sample, 38.5% indicated a family income of "over $80,000" ($N = 60$), with 12.2% reporting $70,000–$80,000 ($N = 19$), 11.5% reporting $50,000–$59,000 ($N = 18$), 9% reporting "under $10,000" ($N = 14$), 7.7% reporting $60,000–$69,000 ($N = 12$), 5.8% reporting $30,000–$39,000 ($N = 9$), 5.8% reporting $20,000–$29,000 ($N = 9$), 5.1% reporting $10,000–$19,000 ($N = 8$), and 4.5% reporting $40,000–$49,000 ($N = 7$).

It is possible that some participants misunderstood what was meant by "family income" and reported their personal income instead. Also, there was a typographical error in this measure creating a scale of categories that are not exhaustive. All end limits should have ended in $999 instead of the even thousand dollar figure. Therefore, although the majority of the sample appears to come from a rather high socioeconomic background, caution must be used in interpreting this information.

## MEASURES

In discussing the measures used in the study, the moderator variables are presented first, then the dependent variables. Moderators included subject expertise, web expertise, and cognitive load. Independent variables include motivation and Internet self-efficacy. Dependent measures included three knowledge measures: factual knowledge, definitional knowledge and knowledge structure (See Appendix C, which contains a summary of the questionnaire).

### *Moderator / Independent Variables*

Subject Expertise

Participants were asked to self-rate their expertise concerning alternative medicine. Specifically they were asked to indicate their level of expertise regarding alternative medicine using a scale ranging from 1 (*novice*) to 10 (*expert*). The mean for this measure was 3.13 ($SD = 1.80$) and 78.9% of the sample ranked their expertise at four and below, which indicates that the sample was relatively unfamiliar with the website content.

Web Expertise

Web expertise was assessed using two questions. First, respondents were asked to indicate how many days they used the WWW in the past week ($M = 6.29$, $SD = 1.33$). Next, they were asked to indicate their perceived expertise using a scale ranging from 1 (*novice*) to 10 (*expert*) ($M = 7.46$, $SD = 1.45$). A composite score was created using these two measures. However, the composite measure seemed problematic for several reasons. The first measure indicating days of use was heavily, negatively skewed. Almost two thirds of the sample (71.0%) indicated using the web every day of the past week. Although transforming this measure into a dichotomy (1 = used everyday, 0 = did not use everyday) solved the skewness problem, it did not seem logical. Also, the two initial measures had a low correlation ($r = 0.25$, $p = .01$). Although

FIGURE 7.   Histogram of Web Expertise (Days of Web Use from the Prior Week)

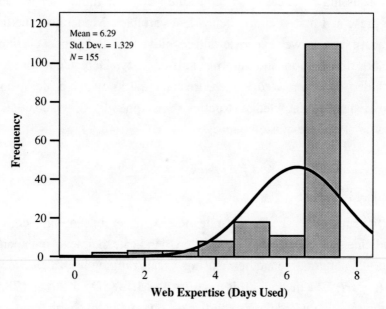

a similar measure has been used successfully in the past (Eveland & Dunwoody, 2001), it was not used in further analysis due to the problems discussed. Instead, the 1 to 10 self-rated web expertise measure was used in this study. The majority of the sample considered themselves relatively high on the expertise measure as 80.9% of the participants ranked themselves at a seven or higher. (See Figures 7 and 8).

## Internet Self-efficacy

The Internet self-efficacy measure was created by adapting items from existing self-efficacy (Eastin & LaRose, 2000; Joo, Bong, & Choi, 2000; Midgley, et al., 2000; Torkzadeh & van Dyke, 2001), expectancy outcome (LaRose, Mastro, & Eastin, 2001) and Internet use (Charney & Greenberg, 2002) measures. Response options ranged from 1 (*strongly disagree*) to 5 (*strongly agree*). The mean Internet self-efficacy score

FIGURE 8.   Histogram of Web Expertise (1–10, Novice to Expert Rating)

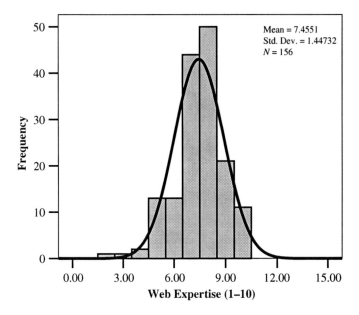

for this sample was 4.48 (*SD* = 0.39), indicating that as a group they were highly self-confident in their abilities to use the Internet. Cronbach alpha for the scale was .93.

Motivation

Intrinsic motivation was assessed using the intrinsic motivation sub-scale of the Situational Motivation Scale (SIMS; Guay, et al., 2000). This measure consists of four items and measures internal motivation toward a task. Response options range from 1 (*corresponds not at all*) to 7 (*corresponds exactly*). The entire scale contains 16 items and four subscales: intrinsic motivation, identified regulation, external regulation, and amotiviation. The scale creators conducted five studies to design and test the scale. They confirmed the factor structure, internal consistency and construct validity of each subscale, and construct validity of the measure. They reported a Cronbach alpha of .95 for the intrinsic motivation subscale. The mean intrinsic motivation score for the current study sample was 3.68 ($SD$ = 1.42), indicating a low to moderately motivated group. Cronbach alpha for this scale in the present study was .92.

## Cognitive Load

Cognitive load is the amount of mental effort exerted when locating and understanding information and its structure. Self-perceived cognitive load was assessed using two different self-report measures. The first measure was a single-item, nine-point measure of mental effort exerted while examining the stimulus website (Paas, 1992; Paas, van Merriënboer, & Adam, 1994). This measure had a mean of 6.28 ($SD$ = 1.16).

The second measure contained four items from Eveland and Dunwoody (2001) and two items constructed from a measure used by Kalyuga, Chandler, Tuovinen, and Sweller (2001). These combined measures focus on understanding of the material but have been used to assess cognitive load in past research. The original version of the Eveland and Dunwoody items used wording that referenced information structured as a story. The items were reworded to focus on general information, such as that which is found on a website. Items were assessed using a five-point response option ranging from 1 (*strongly disagree*) to 5 (*strongly agree*). Eveland and Dunwoody reported an alpha of .79 for this scale. The remaining two items are re-statements of a single item semantic differential-type measure (Kalyuga, et al., 2001). In order to maintain the five-point response option format, the item was reworded to assess the two ends of the dichotomy (very easy and very difficult) as two separate items. The full six-item measure used in this study had a mean score of 1.70 ($SD$ = 0.48) and a Cronbach alpha of .78.

The two cognitive load measures had a moderate negative correlation ($-.31$, $p < .01$), which seems to indicate they are two different concepts—one focusing on mental effort exerted and the other focusing on understanding of the content and how that content is structured. Both measures are discussed in the data analysis section. The multiple item measure is labeled, "cognitive load (misunderstanding) or CLM," and the single item measure is labeled, "cognitive load (effort) or CLE."

*Dependent Variables*

Factual Knowledge

Factual knowledge was operationalized as recognition of content encountered on the stimulus website. It was measured using multiple-choice and true / false questions that relate to the content presented on the stimulus web site. Answers were coded 1 (*if correct*) and 0 (*if incorrect or unanswered*) (Eveland, Cortese, et al., 2004; Eveland, Marton, et al., 2004). Twenty-seven questions (one from each page of the site) were created for this measure. One question had to be deleted from analysis because the content of the question was not reflected in the text from the page it represented. The mean factual knowledge score for this sample was 15.92 ($SD = 2.97$).

Definitional Knowledge

Definitional knowledge was also operationalized as recognition of stimulus site content, but specifically the recognition of term meanings. A matching question format was used to assess definitional knowledge in that the definition of each term was presented with a blank line indicating the missing term. A pull down list of all possible terms allowed participants to choose the correct term for each definition. The pull down list was exactly the same for each question. This measure contained 20 questions, one per specific topic covered in the site. However, one question was phrased incorrectly making it unanswerable. This question was left out of further analysis. As with the factual knowledge measure, answers were coded 1 (*if correct*) and 0 (*if incorrect or unanswered*). This measure had a mean of 11.18 ($SD = 2.89$).

Knowledge Structure Density

KSD was operationalized as the degree of connectedness among concepts. Respondents were given 190 term pairs (representing the 20 topics covered in the stimulus website) for which they indicated the connectedness of each pair of concepts using a scale containing the response options: 0 (*not at all related*) and a range from 1 (*weakly related*) to 4 (*very closely related*; similar measures have been used in Eveland, Cortese, et al., 2004 and Eveland, Marton, et al., 2004). Density was calculated by multiplying all concept pairs by their degree of relatedness, summing them, and then dividing this number by the total number of concept pairs (as used in Eveland, Cortese, et al., 2004; see also Wasserman & Faust, 1994). This type of analysis has emerged from network analysis research. Network analysis focuses on links between elements as a way of examining relationships between these elements (Scott, 1991). The mean knowledge density score for this study was 1.34 ($SD = 0.50$).

## DATA ANALYSIS

Descriptive statistics, Cronbach alpha, correlation, *t*-tests, and general linear model (GLM) analysis were used in this study. All descriptive statistics and Cronbach alpha reliabilities have already been reported to describe the sample and justify scales used in further analysis of the data. For the remainder of the analysis, correlation was used to assess preliminary relationships between the variables. Also, GLM and *t*-tests were used to examine the hypotheses.

# Chapter Three

# Results

Results of the study are presented in this chapter arranged by hypothesis / research question. Before addressing the hypothesized findings, the preliminary relationships among all study variables as indicated by correlation analysis are discussed. Next, results of the GLM analysis of all hypotheses and research questions are discussed. $t$-Tests are used where warranted.

Levene's test of equality of error variances was performed for each analysis reported here. In all cases, the test proved to be non-significant, indicating that homogeneity of variance was confirmed.

## Preliminary Relationships

Of the dependent variables for this study, KSD was not significantly correlated with any other variables and factual knowledge correlated with just one variable, definitional knowledge ($r = 0.55, p < .01$). On the

TABLE 1.    Study One Correlation Table

|          | ISE   | Subj. Exp. | CLE   | CLM    | Mot.  | FK    | DK     | KSD   |
|----------|-------|------------|-------|--------|-------|-------|--------|-------|
| Web Exp. | .50** | .08        | .07   | .02    | .09   | .05   | -.05   | -.04  |
| ISE      |       | .03        | .04   | -.28** | .02   | .07   | .04    | -.04  |
| Subj. Exp. |     |            | .14   | -.07   | .29** | -.06  | -.21** | .14   |
| CLE      |       |            |       | -.31** | .38** | -.01  | .05    | .07   |
| CLM      |       |            |       |        | -.07  | -.11  | -.26** | .02   |
| Mot.     |       |            |       |        |       | -.05  | -.07   | .04   |
| FK       |       |            |       |        |       |       | .55**  | -.07  |
| DK       |       |            |       |        |       |       |        | -.14  |

*Note.* Web Exp. = Web Expertise; ISE = Internet Self-Efficacy; Subj. Exp. = Subject Expertise; CLE = Cognitive Load (Effort); CLM = Cognitive Load (Misunderstanding); Mot. = Motivation; FK = Factual Knowledge; DK = Definitional Knowledge; KSD = Knowledge Structure Density.
**$p < .01$.

other hand, definitional knowledge also had small, negative correlations with cognitive load (misunderstanding, $r = -0.26$, $p < .01$) and subject expertise ($r = -0.21$, $p < .01$).

In examining the independent variables and how they relate to each other, significant moderate relationships were found between Internet self-efficacy and web expertise ($r = 0.50$, $p < .01$) and between motivation and cognitive load (effort, $r = 0.38$, $p < .01$). Also, significant low correlations were found between Internet self efficacy and cognitive load (misunderstanding, $r = -0.28$, $p < .01$) and between motivation and subject expertise ($r = 0.29$, $p < .01$; see Table 1).

## MANIPULATION CHECK

$t$-Tests were used to examine the degree of attention focused on concept definitions and relatedness between concepts as a way to check the effectiveness of the manipulations.

### Definitional Manipulation Check

Participants were asked to indicate how much they paid attention to the definition of each hyperlinked term contained on the website. Response options ranged from 1 (*no attention at all*) to 10 (*very close attention*). *t*-Tests examining reported attention to definitions of concepts proved to be non-significant. Specifically, the reported attention allocation to definitions did not significantly differ between the definitional site condition ($M = 7.00$, $SD = 1.84$, $N = 52$) and the relational site condition ($M = 6.65$, $SD = 1.71$, $N = 52$; $t = 0.994$, $p = .323$, $df = 102$), nor between the definitional condition and the basic condition ($M = 7.08$, $SD = 1.52$, $N = 52$; $t = 0.233$, $p = .816$, $df = 102$).

*Relational Manipulation Check*

Participants were also asked to indicate how much they attended to the connected pages of information as indicated by the relationships specified by the linked concepts. Again, response options ranged from 1 (*no attention at all*) to 10 (*very close attention*). The *t*-test comparing attention to concept relationships between the definitional condition ($M = 7.31$, $SD = 1.58$, $N = 52$) and the relational condition ($M = 7.02$, $SD = 2.07$, $N = 52$) resulted in no significant findings ($t = 0.799$, $p = .426$, $df = 102$). However, the *t*-test comparing attention to concept relationships between the basic ($M = 7.71$, $SD = 1.55$, $N = 51$) and relational conditions indicated marginally significant differences ($t = 1.900$, $p = .060$, $df = 101$).

## SITE DESIGN MANIPULATION AND KNOWLEDGE

Hypothesis one and research question one focused on the three site conditions and whether or not they would have an impact on the three forms of learning. Specifically, they posited that a definitional elaboration site would improve definitional knowledge (*H1a*), a relational elaboration site would improve KSD (*H1b*), and queried which of the three sites (if any) would improve factual knowledge (*RQ1*).

*Definitional Knowledge and Site Design*

Hypothesis 1a stated that a definitional elaboration website design would foster greater definitional knowledge when compared to a relational elaboration website design and a basic nonlinear website design (DefKnow = C + $B$Design). GLM analysis indicated a marginally significant main effect of site condition on definitional knowledge, $F[2, 153] = 2.705$, $p = .070$. To estimate the effects size, $\eta^2$ was used and it indicated that the site design accounted for 3.4% of the variance in definitional knowledge scores.

*t*-Tests were used to directly test the hypothesis that the definitional elaboration site would result in higher definitional knowledge than the other two sites. The *t*-tests indicated that use of the definitional elaboration site resulted in greater definitional knowledge ($M = 11.77$, $SD = 2.75$, $N = 52$) than use of the relational elaboration site ($M = 10.48$, $SD = 3.12$, $N = 52$; $t = 2.234$, $p < .05$, $df = 102$). However, the *t*-test comparing the definitional site to the basic site ($M = 11.29$, $SD = 2.67$, $N = 52$) was not significant ($t = -0.904$, $p = .368$, $df = 102$). See Figure 9

FIGURE 9.    Significant Difference Between the Definitional and Relational Sites for Definitional Knowledge (Hypothesis 1a)

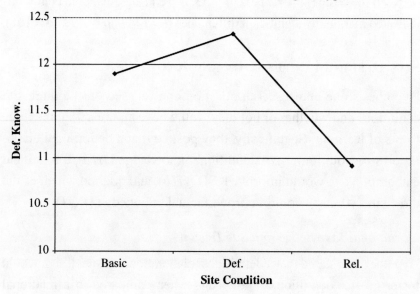

TABLE 2.  Raw Means for Knowledge Measures Across
Site Conditions

| Site Conditions | Definitional Knowledge | | | KSD | | | Factual Knowledge | | |
|---|---|---|---|---|---|---|---|---|---|
| | M | SD | N | M | SD | N | M | SD | N |
| Basic | 11.29 | 2.67 | 52 | 1.33 | 0.51 | 52 | 16.46 | 3.07 | 52 |
| Definitional | 11.77 | 2.75 | 52 | 1.31 | 0.47 | 52 | 15.92 | 2.67 | 52 |
| Relational | 10.48 | 3.12 | 52 | 1.38 | 0.53 | 52 | 15.37 | 3.09 | 52 |

for a visual representation of the differences between means (see also Table 2). Therefore, *H1a* was partially supported.

*Knowledge Structure Density and Site Design*

Hypothesis 1b suggested that a relational elaboration website design would foster greater KSD when compared to a definitional elaboration website design and a basic nonlinear website design (KnowDen = C + BDesign). The GLM analysis of this hypothesis resulted in non-significant main effect findings, $F[2, 153] = .300, p = .742$. Also, individual *t*-tests between the basic ($M = 1.33, SD = 0.51, N = 52$) and relational sites ($M = 1.38, SD = 0.53, N = 52; t = -0.486, p = .628, df = 102$) and the definitional ($M = 1.31, SD = 0.47, N = 52$) and relational sites ($t = -0.768, p = .444, df = 102$) revealed non-significant differences (see Table 2). Therefore, *H1b* was not supported.

*Factual Knowledge and Site Design*

Research Question 1 asked, when comparing three websites (basic, definitional elaboration, and relational elaboration), which will foster more factual knowledge (FactKnow = C + BDesign)? The GLM analysis for this research question resulted in non-significant findings for the main effect of site design ($F[2, 153] = 1.793, p = .170$).

  *t*-Tests were used to compare each website to the other two in order to analyze this research question completely. Non-significant *t*-test results

FIGURE 10.    Significant Difference Between the Basic and Relational
Sites for Factual Knowledge (Research Question 1)

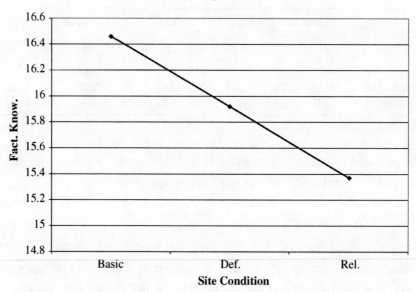

were obtained for the comparisons between the basic ($M = 16.46$, $SD = 3.07$, $N = 52$) and definitional sites ($M = 15.92$, $SD = 2.67$, $N = 52$; $t = 0.954$, $p = .342$, $df = 102$) and for the definitional / relational sites ($t = 0.984$, $p = .327$, $df = 102$). However, the $t$-test comparing the basic site to the relational site ($M = 15.37$, $SD = 3.09$, $N = 52$) was marginally significant ($t = 1.813$, $p = .073$, $df = 102$). See Figure 10 for a graphical representation of mean factual knowledge scores by site condition (see also Table 2).

## SUBJECT EXPERTISE

Subject expertise is discussed in the following section as it relates to definitional, relational, and structural knowledge.

### Definitional Knowledge and Subject Expertise

Hypothesis 2a stated that there would be an interaction between subject expertise and site design such that those low in subject expertise would display higher definitional knowledge when using a definitional elaboration website than when using a basic nonlinear design; whereas those high in subject expertise would display similar definitional knowledge in both the definitional and basic design conditions (DefKnow = C + B design + BSExp + Bdesign * SExp). A GLM analysis was used to test this hypothesis, focusing on only the basic and definitional site conditions. Results indicated that the interaction was not significant, $F[1, 100] = .042$, $p = .838$. Also, a GLM analysis of only the main effects (with the interaction removed) resulted in no significant findings (site condition, $F[1, 101] = 1.218, p = .272$; subject expertise, $F[1, 101] = 1.512$, $p = .222$). Hypothesis 2a was not supported.

Although not hypothesized, a GLM analysis utilizing all three site conditions was used to fully understand the possible relationship between subject expertise, site condition and definitional knowledge. Again, the interaction between site condition and subject expertise was not significant ($F[2, 150] = 1.674, p = .191$). However, an analysis of main effects only revealed significant main effects for site condition, $F[2, 152] = 3.081$, $p < .05$, and subject expertise, $F[1, 152] = 7.661, p < .01$. The definitional site condition resulted in the highest definitional knowledge score when controlling subject expertise (estimated marginal means were: def, $M = 11.87$; basic, $M = 11.17$; rel., $M = 10.50$; see Figure 11). Subject expertise ($b = -.348, t = -2.768, p < .01$) accounted for 4.6% of the variance in definitional knowledge.

*Knowledge Structure Density and Subject Expertise*

KSD was the focus of *H2b*, which stated: There will be an interaction between subject expertise and site design such that those low in subject expertise will display higher KSD when using a relational elaboration website than when using a basic nonlinear design; whereas those high in subject expertise will display similar KSD in both the relational and basic design conditions (KnowDen = C + BDesign + BSExp + BDesign * SExp). GLM analyses focusing on the basic and relational site conditions

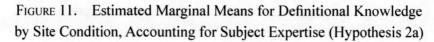

FIGURE 11.    Estimated Marginal Means for Definitional Knowledge by Site Condition, Accounting for Subject Expertise (Hypothesis 2a)

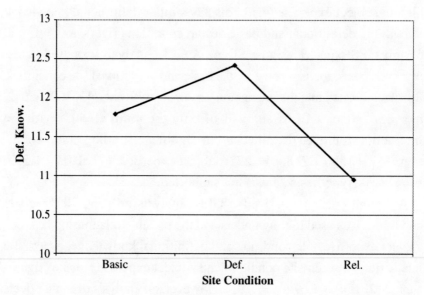

indicated that neither the interaction between site design and subject expertise ($F[1, 100] = 0.003$, $p = .955$) nor the main effects (site condition, $F[1, 101] = 0.123$, $p = .726$; subject expertise, $F[1, 101] = 1.232$, $p = .270$) were significant. Therefore, *H2b* was not supported.

As with definitional knowledge, GLM analyses utilizing all three site conditions were used to examine the relationship between KSD and subject expertise. The interaction between site condition and subject expertise was not significant ($F[2, 150] = 0.087$, $p = .917$), however, there was a marginally significant main effect for subject expertise ($F[1, 152] = 3.332$, $p = .070$) in a separate analysis of main effects. Subject expertise ($b = 0.041$, $t = 1.825$, $p = .070$) accounted for 2.1% of the variance in KSD. The site condition main effect was not significant ($F[2, 152] = 0.370$, $p = .691$).

*Factual Knowledge and Subject Expertise*

Research Question 2 posed the question: Will subject expertise interact with site design (basic, definitional elaboration, and relational elaboration) to increase factual knowledge (FactKnow = C + *B*Design + *B*SExp + *B*Design * SExp)? GLM analyses utilizing all three site conditions were used to answer this question. The analyses revealed non-significant findings for both the interaction between site condition and subject expertise ($F$[2, 150] = 0.507, $p$ = .603) and for both main effects (site condition, $F$[2, 152] = 1.674, $p$ = .191; subject expertise, $F$[1, 152] = 0.352, $p$ = .554).

## WEB EXPERTISE

The findings regarding the effect of web expertise on the three knowledge measures is presented in the section below.

### Definitional Knowledge and Web Expertise

Hypothesis 3a focused on definitional knowledge and web expertise and stated that there would be an interaction between web expertise and site design such that those low in web expertise would display higher definitional knowledge when using a definitional elaboration website than when using a basic nonlinear design; whereas those high in web expertise would display similar definitional knowledge in both the definitional and basic design conditions (DefKnow = C + *B*design + *B*WExp + *B*design * WExp). GLM analyses utilizing data solely from the basic and definitional site conditions resulted in no significant findings for the interaction term ($F$[1, 100] = 1.598, $p$ = .209) nor the main effects (site condition, $F$[1, 101] = 0.797, $p$ = .374; web expertise, $F$[1, 101] = 0.013, $p$ = .910). Therefore, *H3a* was not supported.

GLM analyses containing all site conditions were used to examine the relationship between web expertise and definitional knowledge across all conditions. The interaction term proved to be non-significant in this analysis ($F$[2, 150] = 1.092, $p$ = .338). Also, there was a marginally significant main effect of site condition on definitional knowledge ($F$[2, 152] = 2.737, $p$ = .068) in an analysis of main effects with the interaction term removed.

This finding added further support that the definitional site fosters increased definitional knowledge (estimated marginal means were as follows: def., $M = 11.77$; basic, $M = 11.30$; rel., $M = 10.47$; see Figure 12). A significant main effect of web expertise on definitional knowledge did not emerge from this analysis ($F[1, 152] = 0.510, p = .476$).

*Knowledge Structure Density and Web Expertise*

Hypothesis 3b stated that there would be an interaction between web expertise and site design such that those low in web expertise would display higher KSD when using a relational elaboration website than when using a basic nonlinear design; whereas those high in web expertise would display similar KSD in both the relational and basic design conditions (KnowDen = C + BDesign + BWExp + Bdesign * Wexp). The GLM analyses were limited to the basic and relational site conditions in order to test the stated hypothesis. Results proved to be

FIGURE 12.   Estimated Marginal Means for Definitional Knowledge by Site Condition, Accounting for Web Expertise (Hypothesis 3a)

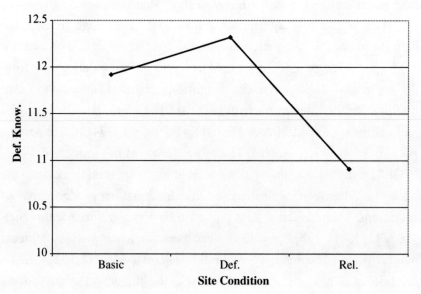

non-significant for both the interaction between KSD and web expertise ($F[1, 100] = 1.017$, $p = .316$) and for the main effects (site condition, $F[1, 101] = 0.209$, $p = .648$; web expertise, $F[1, 101] = 0.104$, $p = .748$), thereby rendering *H3b* unsupported.

GLM analyses utilizing all three site conditions in exploration of the relationship between web expertise and KSD also yielded non-significant results. Both the interaction between site condition and web expertise ($F[2, 150] = 0.541$, $p = .583$) and the main effects (site condition, $F[2, 152] = 0.289$, $p = .750$; web expertise, $F[1, 152] = 0.206$, $p = .651$) were non-significant.

## Factual Knowledge and Web Expertise

A GLM analysis using all three site conditions was used to examine Research Question 3, which asked, will web expertise interact with site design (basic, definitional elaboration, and relational elaboration) to increase factual knowledge (FactKnow = $C$ + $B$Design + $B$WExp + $B$design * WExp)? Neither the model containing the interaction term ($F[2, 150] = 1.906$, $p = .152$) nor the main effects model (site condition, $F[2, 152] = 1.722$, $p = .182$; web expertise, $F[1, 152] = 0.256$, $p = .614$) were significant for this analysis.

## MOTIVATION

Motivation was examined as a main effect for all three knowledge measures. Findings from these analyses are discussed in this section. Hypothesis 4 was not supported in any of the three analyses.

## Definitional Knowledge and Motivation

Hypothesis 4 stated that intrinsic motivation would be positively related to definitional knowledge in all web design conditions (DefKnow = $C$ + $B$intMot + $B$Design). Before testing the stated hypothesis, a GLM analysis examining the interaction between motivation and site design was used to make sure an interaction was not present (thereby validating all assumptions of the GLM analysis). Results indicated no significant findings for an initial examination using the interaction term ($F[2, 150] = 0.026$, $p = .974$), thereby making it possible to examine the main effects. Site condition emerged as a marginally significant main effect ($F[2, 152] = 2.775, p = .066$), however, motivation ($F[1, 152] = 0.891, p = .347$) did not emerge as a significant main effect. Again, the definitional site resulted in the highest definitional knowledge score, even while accounting for motivation (estimated marginal means: def., $M = 11.80$; basic, $M = 11.25$; rel., $M = 10.49$; see Figure 13).

*Knowledge Structure Density and Motivation*

Hypothesis 4 also specified that intrinsic motivation would be positively related to KSD in all web design conditions (KnowDen = C + BIntMot + BDesign). Again, a preliminary analysis using the interaction term was used to test the GLM assumptions. However, a significant interaction

FIGURE 13.    Estimated Marginal Means for Definitional Knowledge by Site Condition, Accounting for Motivation (Hypothesis 4)

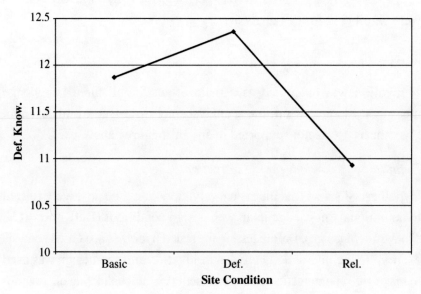

emerged, $F[2, 150] = 3.145, p = .046$ ($\eta^2 = .040$). Further analysis using the traditional Analysis of Covariance (ANCOVA) was not possible because this significant interaction violates its basic assumptions. Therefore, a categorical version of the motivation variable was created. The frequency analysis was used to divide the sample into three groups. Although the intent was to create three equal groups, it was not possible to obtain perfectly equal groups due to the distribution of scores. Motivation was divided into low motivation ($N = 48$), medium motivation ($N = 55$) and high motivation ($N = 53$). An examination of the means produced in the interaction between site condition and motivation indicates that for those using the relational site, the highest mean KSD score was obtained by those who were highly intrinsically motivated ($M = 1.58$; as opposed to the moderately motivated, $M = 1.31$; and the low motivation group, $M = 1.26$). For those using the definitional site, the highest mean KSD score was obtained by the low intrinsically motivated group ($M = 1.49$; moderate motivation, $M = 1.25$; highly motivated, $M = 1.26$). Finally, those using the basic site did not show much difference in terms of mean KSD scores. See Table 3 and Figure 14 for a summary of all findings related to this interaction.

## Factual Knowledge and Motivation

Hypothesis 4 also indicated that intrinsic motivation would be positively related to factual knowledge in all web design conditions

TABLE 3. Mean Knowledge Structure Density Scores for the Site Condition / Motivation Interaction

| Site Conditions | Intrinsic Motivation | | | | | | | | |
|---|---|---|---|---|---|---|---|---|---|
| | Low | | | Medium | | | High | | |
| | *M* | *SD* | *N* | *M* | *SD* | *N* | *M* | *SD* | *N* |
| Basic | 1.35 | 0.54 | 20 | 1.36 | 0.56 | 17 | 1.29 | 0.43 | 15 |
| Definitional | 1.49 | 0.39 | 12 | 1.25 | 0.44 | 19 | 1.26 | 0.53 | 21 |
| Relational | 1.26 | 0.51 | 16 | 1.31 | 0.57 | 19 | 1.58 | 0.47 | 17 |

FIGURE 14.    Interaction Between Motivation and Site Condition
for Knowledge Structure Density

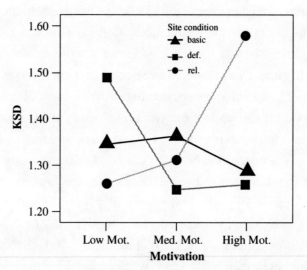

(FactKnow = C + $B$IntMot + $B$Design). An initial GLM analysis was run to examine the interaction between site condition and motivation. The interaction term was not significant in this analysis ($F$[2, 150] = 0.028, $p$ = .972), so it was appropriate to run the analysis examining just the main effects for this model. Both the site condition ($F$[2, 152] = 1.704, $p$ = .185) and motivation ($F$[1, 152] = 0.252, $p$ = .616) main effects were non-significant.

## INTERNET SELF-EFFICACY

Like motivation, Internet self-efficacy was also examined as a main effect on the three knowledge measures. Hypothesis 5 was not supported in the three analyses.

### Definitional Knowledge and Internet Self-Efficacy

Hypothesis 5 predicted that self-efficacy would be positively related to definitional knowledge in all web design conditions (DefKnow = C + $B$ISE + $B$Design). Preliminary analysis revealed a non-significant interaction term between site condition and ISE ($F[2, 150] = 1.187$, $p = .308$). Therefore, it was possible to examine the primary analysis focusing on the main effects of the model. Site condition proved to be a marginally significant main effect, $F[2, 152] = 2.648, p = .074$. As with past analyses, the definitional site prompted the highest definitional knowledge score (estimated marginal means: def., $M = 11.78$; basic, $M = 11.27$; rel., $M = 10.49$; see Figure 15). However, the ISE main effect was non-significant, $F[1, 152] = 0.169, p = .682$.

*Knowledge Structure Density and Internet Self-Efficacy*

Hypothesis 5 also stated that self-efficacy would be positively related to KSD in all web design conditions (KnowDen = $C$ + $B$ISE + $B$Design). The interaction and main effects models were run separately for this analysis. Both the interaction between site condition and ISE

FIGURE 15.    Estimated Marginal Means for Definitional Knowledge by Site Condition, Accounting for Internet Self-Efficacy (Hypothesis 5)

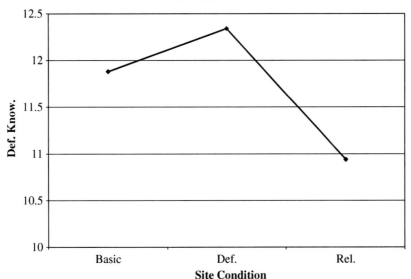

($F[2, 150] = 0.198$, $p = .820$) and the main effects of site condition ($F[2, 152] = 0.284$, $p = .753$) and ISE ($F[1, 152] = 0.190$, $p = .663$) were non-significant.

### Factual Knowledge and Internet Self-Efficacy

Hypothesis 5 also stated that self-efficacy would be positively related to factual knowledge in all web design conditions (FactKnow = $C$ + $B$ISE + $B$Design). The preliminary analysis of the interaction term was not significant ($F[2, 150] = 0.402$, $p = .670$), allowing for further analysis of the main effects using a separate GLM analysis. However, the main effects were also non-significant (site condition, $F[2, 152] = 1.620$, $p = .201$; ISE, $F[1, 152] = 0.373$, $p = .542$).

## COGNITIVE LOAD

As stated earlier, two measures were used to assess cognitive load, one was a single item measure of mental effort exerted and the other was a multiple-item measure of misunderstanding of content and / or content structure. Both measures were used in the following analyses. In each case the mental effort (Cognitive Load Effort, CLE) measure is discussed first and then the misunderstanding (Cognitive Load Misunderstanding, CLM) measure is addressed.

### Definitional Knowledge and Cognitive Load

Hypothesis 6a suggested that there would be an interaction between cognitive load and site design such that those who experience high cognitive load would display lower definitional knowledge when using a definitional elaboration website than when using a basic nonlinear design; whereas those low in cognitive load would display higher definitional knowledge when using a definitional elaboration website than when using a basic nonlinear design (DefKnow = $C$ + $B$Design + $B$CL + $B$design $*$ CL).

Effort as Cognitive Load

Hypothesis 6a was not supported using the CLE measure. This analysis focused on just the basic and definitional site in order to answer the hypothesis. However, both the interaction analysis ($F[1, 100] = 0.016$, $p = .899$) and the main effects analysis (site condition, $F[1, 101] = 0.801$, $p = .373$; CLE, $F[1, 101] = 0.007$, $p = .934$) resulted in non-significant findings.

An examination of CLE across site conditions revealed a non-significant interaction ($F[2, 150] = 0.148$, $p = .863$), but one marginally significant main effect for site condition ($F[2, 152] = 2.648$, $p = .074$) when using a separate analysis with the interaction term removed. Use of the definitional site resulted in the highest definitional knowledge while accounting for CLE (estimated marginal means: def., $M = 11.76$; basic, $M = 11.29$; rel., $M = 10.49$; see Figure 16). The main effect

FIGURE 16.   Estimated Marginal Means for Definitional Knowledge by Site Condition, Accounting for Cognitive Load Effort (Hypothesis 6a)

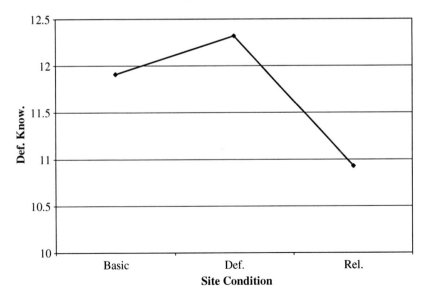

for CLE was not significant in this analysis ($F[1, 152] = 0.369$, $p = .544$).

## Misunderstanding as Cognitive Load

Analyses using the misunderstanding measure of cognitive load also indicated that Hypothesis 6a was not supported. Again, focusing the analyses on just the basic and definitional sites indicated that the inter-action between site condition and CLM was non-significant ($F[1, 100] = 0.926, p = .338$) as were the main effects of site condition ($F[1, 101] = 0.995, p = .321$) and CLM ($F[1, 101] = 2.174, p = .143$) in the main effects model.

It is in the analysis examining the effects of CLM on definitional knowl-edge across site conditions that CLM differs from CLE. This analysis revealed a marginally significant interaction between CLM and site condi-tion ($F[2, 150] = 2.361, p = .098$). CLM had an $\eta^2$ of .028. Because of this significant interaction, it was no longer feasible to use the traditional ANCOVA to examine this relationship. Therefore, the CLM measure was categorized into three (relatively) equal groups. Using the frequency anal-ysis of responses, low ($N = 49$), medium ($N = 46$) and high ($N = 61$) CLM groups were created. The distribution of scores made it impossible to select perfectly equal groups. It is important to note that some of the cells for this analysis are quite small and should be interpreted with caution. The benefit of this analysis is to examine the differences between the means in each group. As is indicated in Table 4 and Figure 17, of those using the relational site, those acquiring the lowest definitional knowledge score were those experiencing high CLM ($M = 9.50$; medium, $M = 10.83$; low, $M = 12.20$). Similarly, for those in the definitional condition, individuals experiencing high CLM obtained the lowest definitional knowledge score ($M = 10.44$), whereas individuals experiencing moderate ($M = 12.53$) and low ($M = 12.42$) levels of CLM were similar in their definitional knowledge scores. Finally, those in the basic condition achieved simi-lar definitional knowledge scores regardless of CLM experienced.

TABLE 4.   Mean Definitional Knowledge Scores for the Site
Condition / Cognitive Load (Misunderstanding) Interaction

| Site Conditions | Cognitive Load (Misunderstanding) | | | | | | | | |
|---|---|---|---|---|---|---|---|---|---|
| | Low | | | Medium | | | High | | |
| | *M* | *SD* | *N* | *M* | *SD* | *N* | *M* | *SD* | *N* |
| Basic | 11.25 | 2.69 | 20 | 11.38 | 2.57 | 13 | 11.26 | 2.86 | 19 |
| Definitional | 12.42 | 2.91 | 19 | 12.53 | 2.61 | 15 | 10.44 | 2.28 | 18 |
| Relational | 12.20 | 2.04 | 10 | 10.83 | 2.85 | 18 | 9.50 | 3.40 | 24 |

FIGURE 17.   Interaction Between Cognitive Load (Misunderstanding)
and Site Condition for Definitional Knowledge

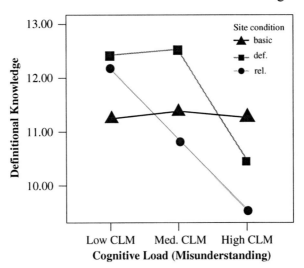

*Knowledge Structure Density and Cognitive Load*

Hypothesis 6b suggested that there would be an interaction between
cognitive load and site design such that those who experience high cognitive load would display lower KSD when using a relational elaboration website than when using a basic nonlinear design; whereas those
low in cognitive load would display higher KSD when using a relational

elaboration website than when using a basic nonlinear design (KnowDen = C + $B$design + $B$CL + $B$design * CL).

## Effort as Cognitive Load

Hypothesis 6b was not supported using the CLE measure. Examining the basic and relational site conditions indicated that both the interaction between site condition and CLE ($F[1, 100] = 0.358, p = .551$), and the individual effects for each (site condition, $F[1, 101] = 0.236, p = .628$; CLE, $F[1, 101] = 1.194, p = .277$), were non-significant. The main effects analysis included only the main effects terms and not the interaction term.

Non-significant results were also obtained in the models containing all three site conditions, which were used to examine the effect of CLE across conditions. The interaction between site condition and CLE was non-significant ($F[2, 150] = 0.470, p = .626$). An analysis containing just the main effects terms also resulted in non-significant findings (site condition, $F[2, 152] = 0.319, p = .727$; CLE, $F[1, 152] = 0.731$, $p = .394$).

## Misunderstanding as Cognitive Load

Use of the CLM measure also indicated that *H6b* was not supported. Using the basic and relational site conditions to test the stated hypothesis, the interaction between site condition and CLM was non-significant ($F[1, 100] = 1.007, p = .318$). The main effect of site condition was also non-significant ($F[1, 101] = 0.221, p = .640$) as was the main effect of CLM ($F[1, 101] = 0.001, p = .979$) in the main effects model.

Again, to fully examine the impact of CLM on KSD, models utilizing all three site conditions were examined. As with earlier analyses, the interaction model ($F[2, 150] = 0.549, p = .579$) and main effects model (site condition, $F[2, 152] = 0.279, p = .757$; CLM, $F[1, 152] = .024, p = .878$) both proved to be non-significant.

*Factual Knowledge and Cognitive Load*

Research question four asked, will cognitive load interact with site design (basic, definitional elaboration, and relational elaboration) to decrease factual knowledge (FactKnow = C + BDesign + BCL + Bdesign $*$ CL)?

Effort as Cognitive Load

All site conditions were utilized in order to examine this research question. However, both models provided non-significant results (interaction, $F[2, 150] = 0.307, p = .736$, site condition main effect, $F[2, 152] = 1.782$, $p = .172$, CLE main effect, $F[1, 152] = 0.010, p = .919$).

Misunderstanding as Cognitive Load

Just as with the effort measure of cognitive load, misunderstanding was analyzed using all three site conditions. The results using CLM were similar to the last analysis in that neither the interaction between site condition and CLM ($F[2, 150] = 0.190, p = .827$) nor the main effects (site condition, $F[2, 152] = 1.449, p = .238$; CLM, $F[1, 152] = 1.243$, $p = .267$) were significant, as indicated in two separate analyses.

## OVERALL MAIN EFFECTS MODELS

This last series of analyses focus on the overall models of main effects for each form of knowledge tested. Two models are presented for each knowledge measure. The first incorporates cognitive load measured as mental effort and the second incorporates cognitive load measured as misunderstanding.

*Definitional Knowledge*

The analysis of definitional knowledge using CLE indicated two significant main effects. There was a marginally significant main effect of site condition on definitional knowledge, $F[2, 148] = 3.002, p = .053$, and a significant main effect of subject expertise on definitional knowledge,

$F[1, 148] = 6.799$, $p < .05$. The definitional site condition resulted in the highest definitional knowledge accounting for all variables (estimated marginal means: def., $M = 11.88$; basic, $M = 11.13$; rel., $M = 10.53$; see Figure 18). Subject expertise ($b = -0.344$, $t = -2.608$, $p < .05$) explained 4.2% of the variance in definitional knowledge (see Table 5).

The model containing CLM resulted in three significant main effects. In addition to site condition ($F[2, 148] = 2.534$, $p = .083$) and subject expertise ($F[1, 148] = 8.101$, $p < .01$), CLM was also a significant main effect ($F[1, 148] = 10.814$, $p < .01$). The definitional site condition (estimated marginal means: def., $M = 11.84$; basic, $M = 11.04$; rel., $M = 10.66$; see Figure 19) resulted in the highest definitional knowledge score when accounting for all predictor variables. Also, subject expertise ($b = -0.364$, $t = -2.846$, $p < .01$) accounted for 4.7%

FIGURE 18.   Estimated Marginal Means for Definitional Knowledge
by Site Condition, Accounting for all Control Variables
(Overall Model Containing CLE)

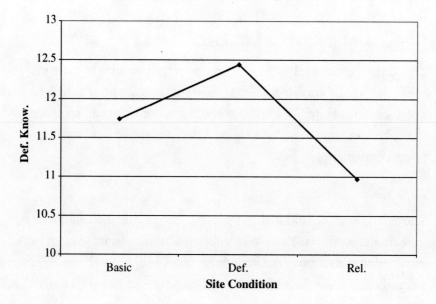

of the variance in definitional knowledge and CLM ($b = -1.615$, $t = -3.288, p < .01$) accounted for 6.2% of the variance in definitional knowledge (see Table 6).

TABLE 5.    Definitional Knowledge Overall Model of Effects, Including Cognitive Load (Effort)

|  | *b (SE)* | *F* | *p* | *df* |
|---|---|---|---|---|
| Site Condition |  | 3.002 | .053 | 2, 148 |
| Subj. Expertise | −0.34 (.13) | 6.799* | .010 | 1, 148 |
| Web Expertise | −0.16 (.18) | 0.785 | .377 | 1, 148 |
| Motivation | −0.10 (.18) | 0.319 | .573 | 1, 148 |
| Self-Efficacy | 0.59 (.67) | 0.784 | .377 | 1, 148 |
| Cognitive Load (Effort) | 0.24 (.21) | 1.353 | .247 | 1, 148 |

*$p < .05$.

FIGURE 19.    Estimated Marginal Means for Definitional Knowledge by Site Condition, Accounting for all Control Variables (Overall Model Containing CLM)

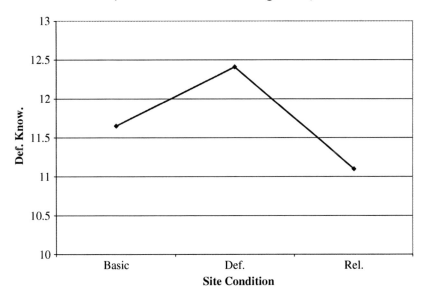

TABLE 6.    Definitional Knowledge Overall Model of Effects,
Including Cognitive Load (Misunderstanding)

| | b (SE) | F | p | df |
|---|---|---|---|---|
| Site Condition | | 2.534 | .083 | 2, 148 |
| Subj. Expertise | −0.36 (.13) | 8.101** | .005 | 1, 148 |
| Web Expertise | −0.04 (.18) | 0.044 | .834 | 1, 148 |
| Motivation | −0.07 (.16) | 0.171 | .680 | 1, 148 |
| Self-Efficacy | −0.12 (.68) | 0.032 | .859 | 1, 148 |
| Cognitive Load (Misunderstanding) | −1.62 (.49) | 10.814** | .001 | 1, 148 |

**$p < .01$.

TABLE 7.    Knowledge Structure Density Overall Model of Effects,
Including Cognitive Load (Effort)

| | b (SE) | F | p | df |
|---|---|---|---|---|
| Site Condition | | 0.369 | .692 | 2, 148 |
| Subj. Expertise | 0.04 (.02) | 3.057 | .082 | 1, 148 |
| Web Expertise | −0.01 (.03) | 0.174 | .677 | 1, 148 |
| Motivation | −0.01 (.03) | 0.043 | .836 | 1, 148 |
| Self-Efficacy | −0.03 (.12) | 0.071 | .790 | 1, 148 |
| Cognitive Load (Effort) | 0.03 (.04) | 0.458 | .500 | 1, 148 |

## Knowledge Structure Density

Both the analyses using CLE and CLM resulted in one significant main effect for KSD, subject expertise. For the CLE model, subject expertise was a marginally significant main effect ($F[1, 148] = 3.057, p = .082$; $b = 0.041, t = 1.748, p = .082$) and explained 2.0% of the variance in KSD. For the CLM model, subject expertise was again marginally significant ($F[1, 148] = 3.193, p = .076; b = 0.042, t = 1.787, p = .076$) and explained 2.1% of the variance in KSD (see Tables 7 and 8).

## Factual Knowledge

Both the model using CLE and the model using CLM indicated no significant main effects (see Tables 9 and 10).

TABLE 8.  Knowledge Structure Density Overall Model of Effects,
Including Cognitive Load (Misunderstanding)

|  | b (SE) | F | p | df |
|---|---|---|---|---|
| Site Condition |  | 0.344 | .709 | 2, 148 |
| Subj. Expertise | 0.04 (.02) | 3.193 | .076 | 1, 148 |
| Web Expertise | −0.02 (.03) | 0.201 | .654 | 1, 148 |
| Motivation | 0.00 (.03) | 0.003 | .959 | 1, 148 |
| Self-Efficacy | −0.02 (.13) | 0.024 | .876 | 1, 148 |
| Cognitive Load (Misunderstanding) | 0.02 (.09) | 0.066 | .798 | 1, 148 |

TABLE 9.  Factual Knowledge Overall Model of Effects,
Including Cognitive Load (Effort)

|  | b (SE) | F | p | df |
|---|---|---|---|---|
| Site Condition |  | 1.429 | .243 | 2, 148 |
| Subj. Expertise | −0.07 (.14) | 0.260 | .611 | 1, 148 |
| Web Expertise | 0.06 (.19) | 0.091 | .764 | 1, 148 |
| Motivation | −0.07 (.19) | 0.153 | .696 | 1, 148 |
| Self-Efficacy | 0.29 (.71) | 0.165 | .685 | 1, 148 |
| Cognitive Load (Effort) | 0.02 (.22) | 0.007 | .931 | 1, 148 |

TABLE 10.  Factual Knowledge Overall Model of Effects,
Including Cognitive Load (Misunderstanding)

|  | b (SE) | F | p | df |
|---|---|---|---|---|
| Site Condition |  | 1.161 | .316 | 2, 148 |
| Subj. Expertise | −0.08 (.14) | 0.336 | .563 | 1, 148 |
| Web Expertise | 0.10 (.20) | 0.277 | .599 | 1, 148 |
| Motivation | −0.08 (.18) | 0.221 | .639 | 1, 148 |
| Self-Efficacy | 0.02 (.75) | 0.000 | .983 | 1, 148 |
| Cognitive Load (Misunderstanding) | −0.61 (.54) | 1.283 | .259 | 1, 148 |

# CHAPTER FOUR

# DISCUSSION

The following chapter details the interpretation of the results found in this analysis. It is organized by hypotheses / research questions, with an initial discussion of some of the preliminary analyses.

## BASIC RELATIONSHIPS BETWEEN VARIABLES

An initial analysis of the relationships between the variables in this study revealed few significant correlations. Findings from this analysis are not discussed in depth as they are meant to be precursors to the more detailed analysis.

Of the dependent variables, only definitional knowledge correlated with some of the independent variables. Specifically, those who easily understood the website content and its structure achieved higher definitional knowledge scores. This relationship is reasonable as we would expect that those who experience high cognitive load to have limited knowledge gain whereas those with low cognitive load would have greater knowledge gain. Also, those with less expertise in alternative medicine achieved higher definitional knowledge scores. This is a curious relationship in that those with subject expertise should have knowledge of the subject area and therefore should obtain higher knowledge scores. Also, factual knowledge and definitional knowledge were moderately related. This relationship is not surprising considering that definitional knowledge and factual knowledge are both recognition measures, whereas KSD is a measure of concept connectedness.

Basic relationships between the independent variables also emerged in this analysis. For instance, high Internet self-efficacy related to high web expertise. This is not a surprising finding as it is reasonable to assume that perceived ability to use the Internet would increase as the user gains experience with the medium. Also, those who understood the content and its structure reported high levels of Internet self-efficacy. This finding is reasonable as those who have confidence in their ability to use the Internet should find it easier to understand the structure of information presented on the Internet as well as the message of that content. Also, those who were more internally motivated to engage in the activity of reading the stimulus website also invested more effort in the task (CLE). Although the CLE measure is meant to measure cognitive load, it places a great deal of emphasis on effort invested in an activity. Therefore, it is reasonable to find that motivation and effort are related to each other. Lastly, those who possessed higher levels of expertise with the subject matter were more highly internally motivated to engage in the web activity. Again, this is an understandable finding in that people who are motivated to gain information in a particular area on their own should also be motivated to engage in a task that contains information from within their area of expertise.

These preliminary analyses are helpful in understanding potential relationships between variables but further analysis was needed to see if these relationships also emerged as causal associations as predicted in the stated hypotheses for this study.

## MANIPULATION CHECKS

The purpose of the definitional and relational sites was to encourage users to elaborate on the concepts presented. The definitional site pop-ups asked users to think about the definition of the linked term and presented that definition just below the request to elaborate. The relational site pop-ups asked users to think about the relationship between the current page's content and the linked term and presented a description of this relationship just below the request to elaborate. These pop-up windows did not present any new information to the user; they just focused attention on specific aspects of the terms.

The manipulation checks indicate that the manipulations used in this study may not have been as strong as originally intended. The definitional manipulation check asked users to indicate, "While using the website, how much did you pay attention to the *definition* of each hyperlinked concept (as indicated by hyperlinked text)?" Responses to this question indicated that users of the definitional site did not focus attention on term definitions more than those using the basic or relational sites. The relational manipulation check asked, "While using the website, how much did you pay attention to how pages of information were *connected to* other pages of information as indicated by the relationships specified by hyperlinked concepts?" Responses indicated that the relational site did not foster increased attention to relationships between concepts when compared to the basic and definitional sites. Actually, when comparing the relational site to the basic site, those using the basic site indicated more self-reported attention to relationships between concepts than those using the relational site. This may suggest that the linked term is enough to encourage elaboration about concept relationships, a finding that is consistent with past research (Eveland, Marton, et al., 2004).

A main function of hyperlinks is to bridge together pieces of information (Morgan, 2002). Therefore, the presence of a link may be enough to stimulate elaboration about concept connectedness.

However, it is not clear whether the mere presence of a linked term should evoke elaboration regarding the definition of that term. Findings regarding these manipulation checks could also be the result of flawed question construction. Perhaps in the wording of the question, too much emphasis was placed on the hyperlinked term, causing those who used the pop-up websites to ignore their presence in the site when answering these questions. Also, another potential explanation could be that the pop-up windows just confused users and caused them not to elaborate. This latter explanation, though possible, should not discredit the use of the definitional pop-ups as use of this site resulted in some significant findings.

## SITE DESIGN AND KNOWLEDGE

The majority of the findings focusing on site design and knowledge resulted in non-significant differences. However, some marginally significant results emerged for definitional knowledge and factual knowledge.

There was a significant main effect of site condition on definitional knowledge, in the GLM model analysis. Individual $t$-tests comparing each site to the other two indicated that use of the definitional site increased definitional knowledge over the relational site, but not when compared to the basic site. This finding is in opposition to what Cress and Knabel (2003) found when comparing the use of previews (pop-up definitional summaries) to no previews. Cress and Knabel noted an increase in knowledge (multiple choice questions based on the site content) when the previews were used. However, Cress and Knabel used a pretest / posttest design to assess knowledge gain, which could account for the differences between their findings and those of the present study. Findings from the present study seem to suggest that the hyperlinked text worked just as well as the definitional pop-ups in focusing attention on the term itself. However, when compared to the relational site, it appears as though the relational pop-ups drew attention away from the term itself. It is too much of an assumption to suggest that the relational pop-ups focused attention on the relationships between terms, but it is certainly feasible to assume that the relational pop-ups drew attention away from the definition of the hyperlinked term.

An overall examination of factual knowledge and site design did not reveal any significant differences. However, a closer look using *t*-tests to compare each site to the other two revealed that factual knowledge was greater for those using the basic site than for those using the relational site, but there were no differences when comparing those using the basic and definitional sites. These findings seem to echo what was found earlier for definitional knowledge. The factual knowledge measure assessed knowledge of pieces of information contained on the site. These pieces of information were not directly related to the term definitions nor to relationships between terms. Again, it would appear that the relational site pop-ups pulled attention from the basic content of the site. This finding appears to be in opposition to what Cress and Knabel (2003) have noted in previous research. Furthermore, past research indicates that more complex designs can hinder factual knowledge. When comparing linear and nonlinear website designs for learning, those using the nonlinear version showed less factual knowledge gain than those using the linear site (Eveland, Cortese, et al., 2004; Eveland, Marton, et al., 2004; see also Eveland, et al., 2002). The current study may add further support to this finding by adding another level of complexity to the examination in the form of pop-up windows.

KSD was not enhanced by the design manipulations. Specifically, the relational pop-up windows did not help to increase the connectedness of concepts as was hypothesized. This finding is in line with Jonassen's past research (1993; and Jonassen & Wang, 1993). In this research, investigators manipulated the navigation structure using pop-up windows, a list of topics, and a graphical map. KSD did not differ across the conditions. Although the current study focuses on only the pop-up window aspect of the Jonassen studies, results are consistent with this earlier work. Conclusions in the earlier studies indicated that structural cues within hypermedia do not automatically result in increased structural knowledge acquisition. This study attempted to go beyond mere structural cues to overt presentation of relational information. However, this also did not result in the expected knowledge structure gain.

Overall, it would appear that when factual knowledge is the goal for learning, a basic hypermedia website is preferable over a pop-up site (when relational information is presented). Also, when definitional knowledge gain is the intended goal, a definitional pop-up site is preferable to a relational pop-up site. These findings add support to previous research indicating that different knowledge measures are important to consider (de Jong & van der Hulst, 2002) and that different hypermedia structures can influence different types of learning (Eveland, Cortese, et al., 2004).

## SUBJECT EXPERTISE

There was not a significant main effect of subject expertise on factual knowledge. However, subject expertise did predict KSD and definitional knowledge.

While controlling the site condition, subject expertise increased KSD. Therefore, in this study it appears as though those with prior expertise in alternative medicine tended to acquire slightly denser structural knowledge on the subject after viewing web content pertaining to alternative medicine. This finding reiterates the basic definition of elaboration and elements of knowledge structure. Elaboration suggests that we build knowledge structure by connecting new information to old, previously acquired information (Schunk, 2000). Through the act of accretion, we add information to our knowledge structure, which becomes denser in the process (Jonassen, 1992).

Also, there were significant main effects of both subject expertise and site condition on definitional knowledge. Subject expertise led to a decrease in definitional knowledge while controlling for site condition. This is a very curious finding. We should expect those with higher subject expertise to know what specific terms mean. Past research indicates that those with high subject expertise have more purposeful navigation patterns (MacGregor, 1999), focusing on new information and avoiding repetition. Perhaps those with subject expertise felt over-confident in their knowledge and did not take the time to fully consider the content of the definitional pop-up windows before clicking out of them. While observing participants during the course of the study, it never appeared as though they clicked out of pop-up windows without reading the content first. However, reading text and thinking about what you read are certainly two different concepts. Also, alternative medicine is an interesting topic to consider when dealing with subject expertise. Some aspects of alternative medicine (such as yoga and herbal remedies) have become more mainstream. So, if a person has experienced a yoga class and tried herbal supplements they assume they know about alternative medicine without realizing the actual depth and breadth of the topic. This may have caused more skimming of the information than was actually warranted. It would have been beneficial to assess subject expertise on several subtopics of alternative medicine. However, the questionnaire was already quite lengthy due to the knowledge structure assessment of 190 term pairs, so this was left out of the questionnaire in order to maintain all of the knowledge structure assessments.

## WEB EXPERTISE

A significant main effect of web expertise did not emerge for any of the three knowledge measures: definitional knowledge, knowledge structure density, or factual knowledge. This is indeed a curious finding as past research indicates that web expertise can lead to increased learning. Even when examining web expertise in relation to print and hypermedia (both linear and nonlinear designs), web expertise has led to increased learning using both forms of presentation (Eveland & Dunwoody, 2001). It is not clear why the current research did not reiterate these past findings.

However, it is important to note that, as Howes and Payne (1990) suggested, skilled web users should be better at locating information than novices, but not necessarily better at gaining information. Although the current study did not use a search task, the findings tend to fall in line with the Howes and Payne article. Yet it is still curious that findings do not coincide with the Eveland and Dunwoody (2001) piece.

Another issue to consider is the concept of web expertise as it was measured in this study. Eveland and Dunwoody (2001) used a composite measure of web expertise in which they combined self-reported expertise and web use in the past month. As noted earlier, the composite measure was problematic in this study for several reasons. First, Eveland and Dunwoody asked participants to indicate their use of the web in the past month, whereas participants in the current study were asked to indicate use in the past week. Second, the weekly use measure resulted in a severely skewed distribution. Third, the web use measure and the self report novice / expert measure shared only a small correlation. Therefore, it is possible that the assessment of web expertise was flawed in this study.

## MOTIVATION

Motivation was predicted to have a direct effect on the three forms of knowledge. This was not the case with factual knowledge and definitional knowledge. However, motivation interacted with site condition in predicting KSD, thereby making the main effects analysis inappropriate.

For those using the basic website, KSD did not differ based on intrinsic motivation. However, KSD differed based on motivation for both the relational and definitional sites.

Specifically, for those using the relational site, highly motivated individuals acquired the most dense knowledge structure, whereas there was not much of a difference between the low and moderately motivated groups. This seems to indicate the importance of motivation in grasping the relationships between concepts. Those who were more interested in engaging the website for personal reasons (intrinsic motivation) were helped by the relational site and this resulted in denser knowledge structures. This finding supports earlier research in which elaboration interacted with motivation to predict KSD (Eveland, Cortese, et al., 2004). However, in the Eveland, et al. study, elaboration was measured and motivation was manipulated, which is the opposite of what was done in this study. This finding is both interesting and exciting as it reveals that the building of knowledge structures appears to take some effort, thereby indicating the importance of motivation in the process. As Jonassen (1993) and Jonassen & Wang, (1993) noted, knowledge structure is not developed merely by the presence of navigational cues. These findings indicate the importance of motivation in prompting an individual to engage relational content, thereby developing KSD.

For those using the definitional site, individuals who were the least motivated acquired the most dense knowledge structure, with not much difference between the medium and high motivation groups. This is a very strange finding. As Hartley (2001) noted, even when considering other factors such as learning strategies, students must be motivated to succeed at their task. So, why were participants successful while not motivated to engage in the task? Or, perhaps even more strange, why weren't participants successful when moderate to highly motivated? Clearly the definitional site hindered knowledge structure gain for motivated participants. Perhaps those who were highly motivated in their task focused very closely on the definitions that were presented in the definitional pop-up windows. This intense focus on the definitions may have hindered there ability to see concept relatedness. Conversely, those who were not motivated to succeed in the task did not focus intently on the definitions, thereby leaving ample resources to make concept relationship connections.

## INTERNET SELF-EFFICACY

Internet self-efficacy was also hypothesized as having a main effect on the three types of knowledge. However, a significant main effect of ISE did not emerge for any of the knowledge measures. Past research has successfully linked self-efficacy to online learning. For instance, Wang and Newlin (2002) noted that students enrolled in an online course had their final exam scores predicted by self-efficacy rather than study habits. The self-efficacy measure used in this study focused on perceived ability to successfully finish the course and to successfully use the web elements of the course. Joo, et al. (2000) also related self-efficacy to learning and found that academic self-efficacy predicted performance on a written exam whereas Internet self-efficacy predicted scores on an Internet search task. These findings add support to the assertion that it is important for researchers to use a self-efficacy measure that reflects the specific task utilized in the research project (Bong & Hocevar, 2002).

This specificity of self-efficacy measurement is most likely the problem with the current study. The self-efficacy measure used in this study focused on a general ability to use the Internet to achieve various tasks such as browsing the Internet, finding specific information, learning specific types of information, and using web pages. It is possible that a more focused measure of self-efficacy was needed for this study. Specifically, a measure addressing perceived ability to understand and learn information presented on the web would have been a better fit.

It was clear at the planning stage of this study that a specific measure of self-efficacy was needed. Although the measure was narrowed beyond basic self-efficacy and beyond computer self-efficacy to Internet self-efficacy, it is evident from the results of these analyses that further specification may have been warranted.

## COGNITIVE LOAD

Cognitive load was analyzed using two different measures. One focused on the amount of mental effort invested in the activity of reading the stimulus website, and the other focused on the difficulty in understanding the presented material and its structure. Both measures were maintained in this study because they clearly measure two different dimensions of the cognitive load construct. Both measures are discussed as they relate to the three knowledge measures.

The CLM and CLE measures had no influence on KSD or on factual knowledge. Analyses focusing on interactions between cognitive load and site condition resulted in non-significant findings as did the analyses focusing on the main effects of cognitive load (using either CLM or CLE) and site condition.

However, findings were different when focusing on definitional knowledge. For cognitive load (misunderstanding), CLM and site condition interacted to predict definitional knowledge. Specifically, those in the relational site who experienced the highest degree of difficulty in understanding the content and its structure acquired the least amount of definitional knowledge, while those experiencing the least amount of difficulty in understanding the content and its structure acquired the most definitional knowledge (those experiencing moderate difficulty understanding the content and structure obtained definitional knowledge between these two scores). This finding was somewhat replicated for those in the definitional site condition. Means did not appear to be greatly discrepant between the low and moderate cognitive load groups, but those experiencing high cognitive load achieved the lowest definitional knowledge score.

These findings are consistent with what is expected from cognitive load theory in that the higher the perceived cognitive load, the less comprehension of material occurs (Macedo-Rouet, et al., 2003). The relational and definitional sites required the most mental effort in order to sort out the information detailed in the pop-up windows (relationships between terms or definitions of terms). Although that information was clearly presented in the pop-ups windows, it required extra elaboration to absorb the information. Perhaps the increased effort needed to understand this information hindered the actual learning of term definitions.

## FACTORS AFFECTING KNOWLEDGE

All variables examined in this study were included in two overall analyses (one using CLE and one using CLM) to examine their effects on the three knowledge measures. In lieu of the earlier analyses throughout this study, it is not surprising that no significant main effects of the independent variables emerged for factual knowledge.

For KSD, subject expertise resulted in more dense knowledge structures. As noted earlier when addressing findings regarding expertise, it was explained that this relationship is in accordance with what we should expect from elaboration and the accretion of knowledge structures. Subject expertise provides a framework for knowledge structure that people can use to make more connections when new information is encountered.

In the examination of definitional knowledge, when all measures were considered, the effect of site condition and subject expertise remained as main effects, although site condition was still only marginally significant. Also, the significant relationship between CLM and definitional knowledge was maintained. These relationships were maintained even when other variables were entered into the overall model examining definitional knowledge.

To address the findings that are upheld here, it would appear that the definitional site helped to increase definitional knowledge. This finding was consistent throughout the study. Of course, the obvious question here is, why did the definitional site manipulation seem to work in this study while the relational site manipulation did not reveal such consistent results? The answer could be in the fact that the definitional pop-up windows provided very clear cut term definitions that were repeated almost word-for-word in the definitional knowledge measure. This was not the case with the relational pop-up windows. Here, the relational pop-ups provided a sentence explaining the relationship between two terms. However, the knowledge structure assessment merely pre-sented pairs of terms and asked participants to indicate their relatedness (or lack of relatedness).

Again, subject expertise decreased definitional knowledge. As noted earlier, this is a curious finding, but may relate to the fact that those with higher subject expertise tend to skim information and this may have hindered their ability to acquire definitional knowledge. Also, in terms of cognitive load, misunderstanding the content and organization of material on the site decreased definitional knowledge. As discussed earlier, this finding is in accordance with cognitive load theory.

## LIMITATIONS

Several possible limitations in this study may have influenced the results reported. Possible limitations are associated with the site manipulations, sample, and measures.

It is possible that the site manipulations used in this study may not have been strong enough to result in an abundance of significant differences, especially with regard to the relational pop-up windows. The pop-up sites were created so that the user was forced to take action

98    INTERNET LEARNING AND THE BUILDING OF KNOWLEDGE

in order to view the requested page. All pop-up windows covered textual information on the current page, making it unreadable. In order to remove the pop-up window subjects could either close the window and go back to the current page or click the link at the end of the pop-up window text to proceed to the requested page. However, even with these use-scenario considerations, it is possible that participants immediately clicked out of a window without reading it. Observations during the course of the study did not indicate that this was a problem, but, this type of analysis was not built into the study, so the possibility of this action must be considered. Furthermore, just because observations indicated that participants did not immediately close the pop-up windows does not necessarily mean that they read the content of those windows while they remained open. Furthermore, reading of the content does not guarantee elaboration of that content. Even though these elaboration conditions were carefully planned, it is difficult to be certain how much "control" we have over human cognition during a research project. However, due to the promising findings regarding the definitional pop-up condition and its influence on definitional knowledge, it appears as though the pop-up window method may be a means of influencing learning. It is the actual content of these pop-up windows that may need further scrutinizing.

A college student sample was chosen for this analysis because they are a prime audience for Internet-based learning. However, college students are also a sample group with a great deal of computer and Internet experience, as indicated in this study. This sample in particular ranked relatively high in terms of web expertise and Internet self-efficacy. Because there was not much variability in either of these measures, it is difficult to note differences based on the level of web expertise and Internet self-efficacy.

Some of the measures from this study, though used successfully in past research, may also have been problematic. For instance, neither cognitive load measure (effort nor misunderstanding) used in this study seemed to fully assess the cognitive load concept. The effort measure was a single item assessing mental effort exerted during the task. It seems as though participants viewed this as effort to do their best and not as cognitive effort invested in the task. On the other hand, misunderstanding was a multiple-item measure that assessed the degree of understanding of the content and how that content was structured. It seems odd to consider understanding as a form of mental effort, however, this measure seemed to get to the concept of cognitive load better than the single item measure as indicated by the findings in this study. The CLM measure appears to assess available cognitive resources as those that remain for deeper processing of information. That deeper process results in compression of the material presented. Further analysis and development of a comprehensive cognitive load measure might be in order for future research. However, of the two assessments used in this analysis, the CLM measure seems the better choice in addressing cognitive load.

## FUTURE RESEARCH

Future research in this area should continue to be focused on how pop-up windows can influence elaboration. As stated earlier, pop-up windows could be problematic, but there is still research to be done in this area. It would be helpful to track usage of such a site to see how long the pop-up windows are actually left open. Taking this a step further, an eye tracking analysis of the site would also help to indicate if people actually attend to the pop-ups when they are open.

The definitional pop-up window manipulation significantly predicted definitional knowledge in this study. As noted earlier, the main difference between the definitional pop-ups and relation pop-ups was that the definitional pop-ups basically previewed the information that was contained in the definitional knowledge measure. This type of preview may have primed users to focus on definitions while viewing the site. It is unclear as to why the same relationship did not emerge between the relational pop-up site and KSD. It could be that the relational information presented in the pop-up windows was too complex for similar priming of the content.

The pop-up windows could also be altered to require an overt action by the user before proceeding to the desired content. Single item quizzes in which the user is asked to fill in a term or choose from a list of answers may help them to think about the issues being addressed. Or, users may even be asked to actually elaborate about concepts in a sentence or two before moving on with their examination of the website.

Also, moving beyond the pop-up window manipulation, perhaps gaming scenarios could be used to foster online learning. A situational game in which a user must create a scenario or character and make choices based on information presented to them about that character or scenario may help them to engage informational content more directly. If forced to make a decision based on information presented one must certainly elaborate on that information first.

Future research should also be focused on the three knowledge measures. Results of this study suggest that definitional knowledge is a distinct form of learning that should be investigated further. Further investigation into how each form of knowledge can be enhanced in the hypermedia environment would be a valuable line of research to follow.

Future research should also focus on KSD in order to understand how it relates to information presented on the web. A major focus of this study was KSD. However, the results of this study were extremely limited with regard to this type of knowledge. In order to examine this particular issue a bit further, a second study was launched focusing solely on KSD as the dependent variable.

# CHAPTER FIVE

# STUDY TWO

The purpose of study one was to understand better the learning process as it relates to information acquired through the WWW. Focus was placed on three types of learning: factual knowledge, definitional knowledge, and knowledge structure (with specific focus on the last two). The site design manipulation used in study one influenced definitional knowledge by encouraging participants to elaborate on term definitions. However, the manipulation to enhance elaboration of concept relatedness did not influence KSD. This is odd as concept relatedness is a core element of elaboration. In lieu of the lack of significant findings related to KSD, study two was undertaken to focus solely on knowledge structure. The purpose of study two was to consider the basic elements and theories of knowledge structure in order to understand how it might be effected (if at all) by web presented information and personal characteristics.

Past research and theoretical pieces on knowledge structure indicate that web presented information should aid in the acquisition of knowledge structure. Hypermedia structure and knowledge structure are thought to be very similar in that they both link pieces of information together. Hypermedia structure is believed to convey appropriate knowledge structures, which could enhance learning (Jonassen, 1992). Research has lent credibility to this assumption in that nonlinear designs have been found to hinder factual learning and free recall, while enhancing KSD (Eveland, Cortese, et al., 2004; Eveland, Marton, et al., 2004; see also Eveland, et al., 2002). However, past research has also cast a shadow of doubt on this link between hypermedia and knowledge structure in that findings have indicated that simply browsing a hypermedia website may not be engaging enough to support meaningful learning in the form of structural knowledge gain (Jonassen, 1993; Jonassen & Wang, 1993). Results from study one fall in line with these latter findings as adding an element of elaboration on concept relatedness also did not lead to structural knowledge gain.

As indicated above, literature linking knowledge structure and hypermedia has been mixed and study one did not further understanding in this area. Therefore, the goal of study two was to bring this evaluation down to its barest elements. Specifically, the study focused on KSD both before and after web exposure to see if a nonlinear web design would indeed alter KSD. Furthermore, this analysis also focused on the personal factors affecting KSD. Therefore, the following research questions were posed:

*RQ1:    Does knowledge structure become denser after exposure to a nonlinear website?*

*RQ2:    Do personal factors such as web expertise, subject expertise, Internet self-efficacy, cognitive load, and motivation influence the denseness of knowledge structure after exposure to a nonlinear website?*

## METHOD

The specific method used for study two is detailed in the following section. First, the procedure and stimulus material are addressed. Next, information about the sample for this study and the measures used are discussed.

### Procedure

The design for this study utilized the Solomon Four-Group Design. This design has been used as a method of handling external validity issues by allowing for generalizability of results (Campbell & Stanley, 1963). Basically four groups are used: a pretest / manipulation / post-test group, a pretest / posttest group, a manipulation / posttest group, and a posttest only group. As Campbell and Stanley noted, because the experimental and control groups do not employ a pretest, it is possible to determine testing main effects and interaction effects between testing and the manipulation. This allows for generalizability as well as the ability to test the manipulation in four different ways.

The Solomon Four-Group Design was chosen for this study because it allows for pre- and post-KSD testing in order to truly examine potential differences in KSD due to the use of hypermedia presented information. The first group (pre / site / post condition) completed a knowledge structure pretest, then examined a nonlinear website, and completed a knowledge structure posttest. The second group (pre / puzzle / post condition) completed a knowledge structure pretest, solved word puzzles, and then completed a knowledge structure posttest. The third group (site / post condition) examined a nonlinear website then completed the knowledge structure posttest. The fourth group (puzzle / post condition) solved word puzzles then completed the knowledge structure posttest. This design allows for four important comparisons to confirm differences between the pre- and post-knowledge structure measures for the pre / site / post condition. (See Figure 20).

FIGURE 20.    Solomon Four-Group Design Used in Study Two

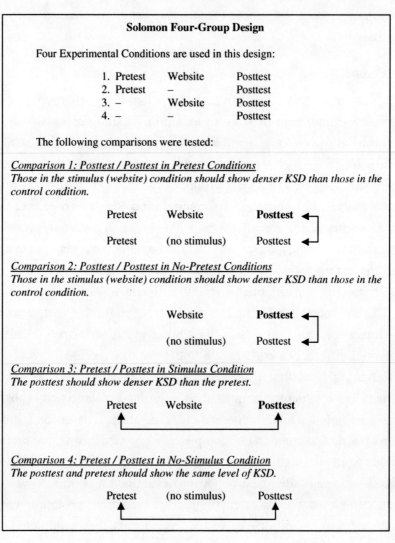

Participants were randomly assigned to one of four experimental groups upon arrival at the testing area. The entire study was accessible online. Participants were first asked to indicate acceptance of the consent form. Next, they received a pretest questionnaire that measured subject expertise, web expertise, Internet self-efficacy, and demographic information. Those in the two pre / post conditions also answered knowledge structure questions while those in the post only conditions were immediately directed to online instructions leading them to a site containing word puzzles. Once everyone had finished the pretest, all participants were handed instructions leading them to the next portion of the study. Those in the site conditions were asked to examine a non-linear site pertaining to alternative medicine, while those in the puzzle conditions were directed to a different word puzzle site. Participants were asked to examine the website / solve word puzzles for approximately 20 minutes. (See Appendix D for full instructions). After the exposure session ended, participants answered a posttest questionnaire consisting of measures of motivation, cognitive load, and knowledge structure.

*Stimulus*

Just as with study one, a website containing health information focusing on alternative medicine (i.e., acupuncture, acupressure, herbs, massage, yoga, meditation, detoxification, etc.) served as the stimulus material for this study. The site used for this study was the control ("basic") site from study one. This website is detailed in the methods section of study one. (Figure 4 is a sample page from the site).

*Sample*

The sample for study two consisted of 208 undergraduate students from a large Midwestern university. Participants were recruited from communication courses and they were offered extra course credit for their participation. The same demographic questions for study one were used in study two.

In terms of age and gender the sample tended to be female and in their early twenties. Specifically, ages ranged from 18 to 34 years, with an average age of 21.62 years ($SD = 2.56$). Also, the majority of the sample was female (65.4%, $N = 136$) as opposed to male (34.6%, $N = 72$).

Regarding race, the majority of the sample indicated that they consider themselves to be Caucasian / White (82.7%, $N = 172$). Also, 10.1% consider themselves to be African–American ($N = 21$), 6.3% indicated Asian–American ($N = 13$), and 0.5% indicated that they were Hispanic ($N = 1$). Eight participants (3.8%) indicated their race as "Other." Five of the participants left the open-ended portion that accompanied the "Other" category blank, while two participants indicated that they were Native-American and the last indicated their race as Ethiopian.

The assessment of current class standing (or class rank) revealed that the majority of the sample consisted of seniors (61.4%, $N = 127$), with the remaining groups as follows: 20.3% were juniors ($N = 42$), whereas 10.1% were sophomores ($N = 21$) and 8.2% were freshmen ($N = 17$).

Not surprisingly, the majority of the sample reported their marital status as single (96.6%, $N = 201$). Five participants reported being married (2.4%), one was divorced (.5%), and one was separated (.5%).

Finally, in terms of income, the modal income reported by this sample was $70,000–$80,000. The majority of the sample, 40.9% indicated a family income of "over $80,000" ($N = 83$), with 9.4% reporting $70,000–$80,000 ($N = 19$), 9.4% reporting $30,000–$39,000 ($N = 19$), 8.4% reporting $50,000–$59,000 ($N = 17$), 7.9% reporting "under $10,000" ($N = 16$), 6.9% reporting $40,000–$49,000 ($N = 14$), 6.4% reporting $60,000–$69,000 ($N = 13$), 5.4% reporting $20,000–$29,000 ($N = 11$), and 5.4% reporting $10,000–$19,000 ($N = 11$). Unfortunately, a problem with this measure from study one was inadvertently carried over into study two in that the categories are not exhaustive because they end in "000" and not "999."

*Measures*

Measures used for this study include the knowledge structure assessment, which was used as a pre- and posttest measure and personal factors which were used as independent variables. Independent variables include subject expertise, web expertise, Internet self-efficacy, motivation, and cognitive load. (See Appendix E for summaries of the pre- and post-questionnaires).

Pre / Post-Knowledge Measure

Knowledge structure was assessed before presentation of the stimulus site for half of the sample and after presentation of the stimulus site for the entire sample. Distracter items were added to the pretest in order to control for the possible influence of previewing questions from the posttest.

**Knowledge Structure Density.** KSD is the degree of connectedness among concepts. This measure is described in the methods section of study one. Fifty-five pairs of terms were added to the pretest as distracter items. These fifty-five pairs compared the relatedness of health topics not covered in the main KSD assessment (i.e., heart disease, high blood pressure, obesity, chronic pain, allergies, emphysema, smoking, drinking alcohol, exercise, stress, and nutrition). Density was then calculated using the 190 pairs of core concepts that related to the alternative medicine site. The mean knowledge density score for this study was 1.25 ($SD = 0.51$, $N = 104$) for the pretest measure and 1.35 ($SD = 0.65$, $N = 208$) for the posttest measure.

Independent Variables

The personal factors that were used as independent variables in study two include subject expertise, web expertise, Internet self-efficacy, motivation, and cognitive load. The measures used to assess these variables in study one were also used in this study. Full descriptions of these measures can be found in the method section for study one. In two cases where multiple measures were used to assess the concept of interest (web expertise and cognitive load), just one measure was retained for study two. This is discussed further below.

Although descriptions for the various redundant measures can be found in study one, the means calculated for each measure used in study two are presented here. This sample obtained a mean subject expertise score of 3.28 ($SD$ = 1.97). The mean score for Internet self-efficacy was 4.46 ($SD$ = 0.45). The Cronbach alpha for the ISE scale was .94. The mean intrinsic motivation score for the current study sample was 3.76 ($SD$ = 1.47), indicating a low to moderately motivated group. Cronbach alpha for this scale in study two was .93.

*Web Expertise.* Web expertise was assessed using one question that assessed perceived expertise using a scale ranging from 1 (*novice*) to 10 (*expert*). Although two measures of web expertise were used in study one, only this measure was actually retained for further analysis as there appeared to be problems with the other measure (assessing days of web use during the prior week). Therefore, only the 1–10 web expertise measure was retained for study two. The average web expertise score for this sample was 7.31 ($SD$ = 1.56).

*Cognitive Load.* Two measures of cognitive load were used throughout study one. One assessed mental effort exerted during a task and the other assessed understanding of web content and its structure. Due to the extremely long nature of the study two questionnaires (because of the KSD term pairs that some participants considered twice), only the mental effort measure of cognitive load was used in study two because it is a single item measure. At the time of this decision, the cognitive load measures from study one had not been fully analyzed. In hindsight, perhaps it may have been beneficial to include the misunderstanding measure instead of the effort measure as it seemed to lead to more interesting findings in study one. However, the choice was made based on questionnaire length and therefore seemed reasonable at the time. This measure had a mean of 6.34 ($SD = 1.52$) in study two.

## DATA ANALYSIS

Analyses for this study include descriptive statistics, Cronbach alpha, correlation, *t*-tests, ANOVA and regression analysis. All descriptive statistics and Cronbach alpha reliabilities have already been reported to describe the sample and justify scales used in further analysis of the data. For the remainder of the analysis, correlations were used to assess preliminary relationships between the variables used in this study, *t*-tests were used to examine differences between the four experimental groups (with further analysis using ANOVA), and regression was used to analyze the impact of the independent variables on KSD.

## RESULTS

Results of study two are detailed in this section. First the preliminary relationships between variables are presented, then the analyses associated with the two research questions for this study are discussed.

As with study one, a Levene's test of equality of error variances was performed for each analysis reported here (where appropriate). In all cases, the test proved to be non-significant, indicating that homogeneity of variance was confirmed.

### Preliminary Relationships

In order to examine preliminary relationships between post-KSD and all other variables, correlation analyses were run using the whole sample and each of the four experimental conditions. Pre- and post-KSD were significantly correlated in all possible conditions (whole sample, $r = 0.56, p < .01$; pre / site / post, $r = 0.30, p < .05$; pre / puzzle / post, $r = 0.85, p < .01$).

TABLE 11.    Study Two Correlations Between All Variables
and Post-Knowledge Structure Density Using the Whole
Sample and Each Experimental Condition

|  | Whole Sample | Pre / Site Post | Pre / Puzzle Post | Site / Post | Puzzle / Post |
|---|---|---|---|---|---|
| Web Exp. | -.03 | .10 | .03 | -.18 | -.10 |
| ISE | -.13 | -.15 | -.09 | -.14 | -.13 |
| Subj. Exp. | .11 | .13 | .07 | -.17 | .43** |
| CLE | .14* | .24 | .04 | -.10 | .33* |
| Mot. | .02 | .16 | .11 | -.28* | -.06 |
| Pre-KSD | .56** | .30* | .85** | – | – |

*Note.* Web Exp. = Web Expertise; ISE = Internet Self-Efficacy; Subj. Exp. = Subject Expertise; CLE = Cognitive Load (Effort); Mot. = Motivation; Pre-KSD = Pre Knowledge Structure Density.
*$p < .05$. **$p < .01$.

Cognitive load had a low positive correlation with post-KSD when examining the whole sample ($r = 0.14, p < .05$) and a moderate positive correlation when focusing on the puzzle / post condition ($r = 0.33, p < .05$). Subject expertise had a moderate positive correlation with post-KSD in the puzzle / post condition ($r = 0.43, p < .01$). Finally, motivation had a moderate negative correlation with post-KSD in the site / post condition ($r = -0.28, p < .05$; see Table 11 for a report of all correlations observed in these analyses).

Among the independent variables, all relationships were low to moderate. Internet self-efficacy and web expertise ($r = 0.46, p < .01$) and cognitive load and motivation ($r = 0.37, p < .05$) each had moderate positive correlations. At the same time, subject and web expertise had a low positive correlation ($r = 0.14, p < .05$; see Table 12).

*Pre / Post-Knowledge Structure Density*

Research question one posed the question: Does knowledge structure become denser after exposure to a nonlinear website? The Solomon Four-Group Design was used to examine this research question. According to this design, four important tests must be evaluated to

TABLE 12.    Study Two Independent Variable
Correlation Table

|            | ISE   | Subj. Exp. | CLE  | Mot.  |
|------------|-------|------------|------|-------|
| Web Exp.   | .46** | .14*       | .04  | .09   |
| ISE        |       | .06        | −.01 | .13   |
| Subj. Exp. |       |            | .10  | .13   |
| CLE        |       |            |      | .37** |

*Note.* Web Exp. = Web Expertise; ISE = Internet Self-Efficacy; Subj. Exp. = Subject Expertise;
CLE = Cognitive Load (Effort).
*$p < .05$. **$p < .01$.

determine if there is indeed a significant change from the pre to post measure (See Figure 20).

First, comparisons between the posttests (comparisons 1 and 2) were analyzed. Comparison 1 examined the posttests for the two pretest conditions. The KSD posttest in the site condition ($M = 1.66$, $SD = 0.73$, $N = 52$) was significantly higher than the KSD posttest in the puzzle condition ($M = 1.13$, $SD = 0.63$, $N = 52$; $t = 3.967$, $p < .001$, $df = 102$). Comparison 2, on the other hand, examined the posttests for the two conditions without the pretest. For this comparison, the KSD posttest in the site condition ($M = 1.35$, $SD = 0.57$, $N = 53$) was not significantly different from the KSD posttest in the puzzle condition ($M = 1.27$, $SD = 0.56$, $N = 51$; $t = 0.673$, $p = .503$, $df = 102$).

Second, comparisons between the pre- and posttests (comparisons 3 and 4) were analyzed. Paired sample $t$-tests were used because the pre- and posttests did not come from independent samples. In the site condition, the KSD pretest ($M = 1.33$, $SD = 0.53$, $N = 52$) was significantly lower than the KSD posttest ($M = 1.66$, $SD = 0.73$, $N = 52$; $t = -3.120$, $p < .01$, $df = 51$). In the puzzle condition, the KSD pretest ($M = 1.18$, $SD = 0.49$, $N = 52$) was not significantly different from the KSD posttest ($M = 1.13$, $SD = .63$, $N = 52$; $t = 1.163$, $p = .250$, $df = 51$; see Figure 21).

FIGURE 21.    Solomon Four-Group Analysis Results

**Solomon Four-Group Design**

Four Experimental Conditions are used in this design:

| | | | | |
|---|---|---|---|---|
| 1. | Pretest ($M = 1.33$) | Website | Posttest ($M = 1.66$) |
| 2. | Pretest ($M = 1.18$) | – | Posttest ($M = 1.13$) |
| 3. | – | Website | Posttest ($M = 1.35$) |
| 4. | – | – | Posttest ($M = 1.27$) |

The following comparisons were tested:

*Comparison 1: Posttest / Posttest in Pretest Conditions*
*Those in the stimulus (website) condition should show denser KSD than those in the control condition.*

Pretest        Website        **Posttest**
                                    $t = 3.967***$
Pretest        (no stimulus)  Posttest

*Comparison 2: Posttest / Posttest in No-Pretest Conditions*
*Those in the stimulus (website) condition should show denser KSD than those in the control condition.*

Website        **Posttest**
                            $t = .673$
(no stimulus)  Posttest

*Comparison 3: Pretest / Posttest in Stimulus Condition*
*The posttest should show denser KSD than the pretest.*

Pretest        Website        **Posttest**
                                    $t = -3.120**$

*Comparison 4: Pretest / Posttest in No-Stimulus Condition*
*The posttest and pretest should show the same level of KSD.*

Pretest        (no stimulus)  Posttest
                                    $t = 1.163$

$**p < .01, ***p < .001$.

Based on the findings here, it appears as though there may be an interaction between the pretest and the stimulus material. This is an issue discussed by Campbell and Stanley (1963) as a threat to external validity. They suggested that it is possible for a pretest measure to influence results in a posttest because of a sensitization to the material encountered. As it applies to this study, individuals may have been sensitized to the relationships between alternative medicine terms and therefore more aware of them while using the stimulus website. An ANOVA analysis examining the interaction between the pretest and the stimulus was necessary to investigate this possibility further.

A 2 × 2 ANOVA indicated that the interaction significantly predicted posttest KSD ($F[1, 204] = 6.818, p < .05$). The interaction accounted for 3.0% of the variance in KSD. The highest mean KSD score emerged from the pretest / site condition ($M = 1.66$) indicating that the pretest primed participants on the term relationships before they viewed the site. Alternatively, the lowest mean KSD score was achieved by those who took the pretest, but did not view the site ($M = 1.13$). The two "no pretest" conditions resulted in mean KSD scores between these two

FIGURE 22.   Interaction Between Stimulus and Pretest
in Predicting Knowledge Structure Density

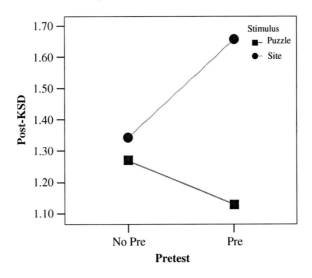

extremes (site, $M = 1.35$; puzzle, $M = 1.27$; see Figure 22 for a graphical representation of this interaction).

*Personal Factors and Knowledge Structure Density*

Research question two asked: Do personal factors such as web expertise, subject expertise, Internet self-efficacy, cognitive load, and motivation influence the denseness of knowledge structure after exposure to a non-linear website? A regression analysis was used to answer this question. The site variable, pretest variable and interaction term were entered into the model in step one of the regression. These variables accounted for 8.8% of the variance in KSD ($F[3, 206] = 6.520, p < .001$). Next, the personal factor variables were added in step two of the regression. All of the variables in this model accounted for 13.4% of the variance in KSD ($F[8, 206] = 3.815, p < .001$). While controlling for site, pretest and the interaction between the two, three variables emerged as significant predictors of KSD. The site / pretest interaction variable ($\beta = .255$) had a low, positive relationship with KSD. Subject expertise ($\beta = .123$) and cognitive load ($\beta = .135$) also had low, positive relationships with KSD, but these findings were marginally significant (see Table 13 for the details regarding this analysis).

## DISCUSSION

The purpose of study two was to gain insight into KSD as it relates to hypermedia use. Findings from this study are addressed in terms of preliminary relationships, pre / post-KSD, and independent variables as they relate to post-KSD.

*Preliminary Relationships*

Preliminary correlation analysis indicated that pre- and post-KSD are positively related. This relationship is not surprising as knowledge structure is something that is fine tuned and restructured but not

TABLE 13. Multiple Regression
for Variables Predicting Knowledge
Structure Density

| Variables | β | t |
|---|---|---|
| Step 1 | | |
| Site | .05 | 0.507 |
| Pretest | −.12 | −1.250 |
| Site Pretest* | .31 | 2.675*' |
| Step 2 | | |
| Site | .10 | 1.004 |
| Pretest | −.07 | −.717 |
| Site Pretest* | .26 | 2.144* |
| Web Expertise | .00 | 0.035 |
| Subject Expertise | .12 | 1.802[a] |
| Internet Self-Efficacy | −.12 | −1.564 |
| Intrinsic Motivation | −.03 | −0.436 |
| Cognitive Load | .14 | 1.848[b] |

*Note.* Step 1: $R = .30$, $R^2 = .09$, $\Delta R^2 = .07$, $F[3, 206] = 6.520$, $p < .001$;
Step 2: $R = .37$, $R^2 = .13$, $\Delta R^2 = .10$, $F[8, 206] = 3.815$, $p < .001$.
[a] Marginally significant at .073.
[b] Marginally significant at .066.
*$p < .05$. **$p < .01$.

replaced by new knowledge (Jonassen, 1988; 1993; Jonassen, et al., 1993). What is especially interesting in these preliminary analyses is that pre- and post-KSD were most highly correlated in the condition that did not contain the stimulus site, while a lower correlation was noted for the condition containing the stimulus site. Even at the preliminary analysis stage this finding hints at the important impact of the stimulus site in changing KSD. Also, post-KSD was positively related to cognitive load when examining the full sample and when examining the posttest only condition. It is interesting that those who invested a high amount of mental effort in solving word puzzles also had dense post-KSD. This finding may relate back to what was noted in study one in that CLE was viewed as effortful engagement in a task. Perhaps those who invested a great deal of effort in solving the word puzzle had this effort carried over into their post-KSD assessment and they more actively made connections between terms. Subject expertise was also correlated to post-KSD in the posttest only condition. This is a very odd finding. If subject expertise is truly related to post-KSD, the significant correlation should have emerged in all conditions. The final significant correlation indicated that those with low intrinsic motivation had denser knowledge structures when in the posttest only condition. This is another very strange finding as motivation should increase KSD. It is possible that participants were motivated to read the site and even absorb information from it, just not information pertaining to concept relatedness.

Relationships between the independent variables indicate that perceived ability to use the Internet successfully related to expertise using the web. This echoed the basic relationship found in study one. Also, cognitive load and motivation were positively correlated indicating a possible link between effort and motivation. This relationship points to a possible problem with cognitive load as a self-reported measure of effort invested. It appears to be viewed as a personal effort put forth by the individual to invest effort in a task and not as a measure of cognitive resource allocation. Finally, there was a low correlation between subject and web expertise indicating that those familiar with using the web were also familiar with the subject matter for this study.

*Pre / Post-Knowledge Structure Density*

Three of the four comparisons detailed in the Solomon Four-Group Design were significant and in the intended direction. First, comparing the post-KSD measures in the pre / site / post and pre / puzzle / post conditions should have revealed a significant difference between the post measure in the site condition and the post measure in the puzzle condition. This indeed was the case as the site condition post-KSD was significantly denser than the puzzle condition post-KSD. This finding indicates that the site influenced post-KSD. In the second comparison, post-KSD should have been higher in the site / post condition than in the puzzle / post condition. Significant differences were not revealed in this comparison. This finding sheds some doubt on the significant findings from comparison one, indicating that the site may not have been as influential as first thought. Third, within the pre / site / post condition, pre-KSD should have been lower than post-KSD. Findings were in the anticipated direction indicating that post-KSD was significantly denser than pre-KSD after exposure to the website stimulus. However, this finding combined with the second comparison may indicate that it was the pre-KSD measure and not the site that made post-KSD denser. The fourth comparison is within the pre / puzzle / post condition and compared the pre- and post-KSD measures. In this comparison, the premeasure should have been the same as the post. This proposed relationship was found in the analysis as the pre- and post-KSD measures were not significantly different from each other.

Therefore, taken together, it appears as though we have some support for the finding that hypermedia presented information influences KSD. However, because not all comparisons detailed in the Solomon Four-Group Design were in the intended direction, this conclusion must be interpreted with caution and requires further analysis. If this is indeed the case, though, it echoes past findings that nonlinear hypermedia designs foster greater KSD (Eveland, Cortese, et al., 2004; Eveland, Marton, et al., 2004), a finding that did not emerge in study one.

Based on the findings from the Solomon Four-Group Design analysis, it was important to examine whether or not there was an interaction between the pretest and the stimulus website in predicting KSD. An ANOVA indicated that this was the case. Specifically, the pretest primed individuals to think about the relationships between concepts as they viewed the stimulus website. This resulted in denser KSD for those who both took the pretest and examined the stimulus website. Past research has indicated that KSD can be influenced by concept association tasks after examination of content material (Jonassen, 1993; Jonassen & Wang, 1993). However, this finding adds a different element to the understanding of KSD—that we may be able to help prime structural knowledge learning by making subjects think about concept relationships before the content material is viewed.

The findings from study two are in synch with some of the findings from study one. Specifically, a major finding in study one was that the definitional elaboration site led to greater definitional knowledge. As indicated in the discussion of study one findings, the definitional pop-up windows restated definitions that were used in the definitional knowledge measure. Furthermore, these definitions were very clear and simple to understand. Therefore, it is possible that participants were primed by the definitional pop-ups to further attend to the definitions that were presented in the website (not necessarily presented as restatements in the text of the website, but very similar wording was used). This may then have led to improved definitional knowledge. A similar trend was noted in study two related to KSD. Specifically, the pretest (which was a restatement of the posttest) primed participants to focus on the relationships between concepts as presented within the website (which were not restatements of the term comparisons used in the pre- and posttests). This priming then led to denser post exposure KSD.

This finding, now emerging in two studies for two different stimuli and two different forms of knowledge gain, may be a viable area for future investigation in the realm of learning from the WWW. Priming WWW users to focus on particular kinds of information appears to bolster that particular type of knowledge gain. It appears as though the key may be in making sure the priming content matches the end assessment measure.

*Independent Variables and Post-Knowledge Structure Density*

There is some indication that subject expertise and cognitive load also predict KSD. Specifically, the more subject expertise an individual has, the denser their KSD. This same finding was noted in study one, thereby adding further support to the connection between subject expertise and KSD. This finding is in accordance with the basic concepts of KSD and elaboration in that we should expect those with background knowledge in a specific topic to develop, and continue to develop, their knowledge structure in this area. As stated earlier, knowledge structures are not replaced, but restructured and further developed (Jonassen, 1988, 1993; Jonassen, et al., 1993).

Also, results of this analysis revealed that those experiencing high cognitive load had denser knowledge structures. This is an odd finding as one would expect cognitive load to interfere with learning. However, when the measure of cognitive load that was used in this study is evaluated further, it indicates that this particular measure assessed personal reports of mental effort invested in the task. It is possible that participants interpreted this as an effort to succeed in the task. If this is the case, those that tried harder to succeed, did in fact obtain denser knowledge structures, a finding that makes much more sense. Issues with this measure were discussed in study one. However, what this finding indicates is that developing structural knowledge is an effortful process. Those who are willing to invest the effort, realize the rewards. Although the CLE measure was also used in study one, no significant findings emerged in that analysis.

## LIMITATIONS

As with study one, limitations for this study also fall into the areas of sample and measures used. Again, college students were used as the sample for this study because they are the primary audience for online learning. However, this sample consisted of participants who were very knowledgeable about using the web and highly self-efficacious about their ability to use the web.

Also, as noted in study one, certain measures may not be ideal for the concept they are intended to measure. As mentioned above, the cognitive load measure may not assess mental effort, but overall effort invested in completing a task. Another limitation is associated with the knowledge structure measure. Rating several item pairs can be very tedious, especially for the pretest / posttest groups who ranked 245 pairs (190 pairs for analysis plus the 55 distracter items) in the pretest and 190 pairs in the posttest.

## FUTURE RESEARCH

Future research should continue to examine the concept of knowledge structure. Perhaps more detailed analyses between the density of website topic connections and KSD would help to connect the concept of KSD more closely to web structures. It might also help to actually look at some of the specific nodes that are connected in the human knowledge structure as it compares to specific nodes of hyperlinked content on a web page. Jonassen (1988) noted that hypermedia could be seen as a tool for displaying *appropriate* knowledge structures with the hope of duplicating these structures on the knowledge structures of learners.

Although the knowledge structure measure seemed to work fine in both study one and study two, it might be beneficial to find a way to assess knowledge structure so that it is not so tedious a task. Observations during the course of both studies indicated that, although participants were willing to fully participate in the study by examining all the relational pairs and making assessments about them, they seem to get a little bored or tired during the process. However, nothing was witnessed during this study to prompt the researcher to assume that some of the findings regarding this measure were invalid.

Research is also needed in examining what factors might influence KSD. This study added some information as to the influence of subject expertise and cognitive load (mental effort) on KSD. Further analysis into both of these concepts is advisable. Sorting out issues regarding cognitive load and how it should be measured may result in different ways of assessing cognitive load as it relates to KSD. Also, in examining subject expertise, it might be helpful to look at specific subareas of expertise within a given topic to see how they relate to KSD, perhaps by segmenting KSD based on the subareas of expertise. It would also be valuable to understand what other variables may impact KSD. For instance, learning styles or intelligence quotients could be important in understanding KSD.

## OVERALL CONCLUSIONS

The majority of the significant findings from the research detailed here focus on definitional knowledge. The definitional elaboration site had some success in increasing definitional knowledge (when compared to the relational site but not the basic site), even when factoring personal characteristic variables into the model as main effects. Also, factual knowledge was enhanced by the basic (control) site (when compared to the relational site but not the definitional site). Study one indicated that neither of the site manipulations nor the basic site aided KSD.

However, study two was able to add some insight into how KSD may be enhanced. Specifically, exposure to the pretest KSD measure primed participants to focus on website content more closely thereby resulting in denser KSD. A similar priming effect was also noted in relation to definitional knowledge in study one. These findings indicate that when content from the posttest is restated and presented before exposure to hypermedia content it can help to focus that exposure and increase knowledge gain. This finding is in accordance with research on encoding specificity (Lachman, et al., 1979). When recall cues match information encountered during the encoding process, retrieval success is greater (Tulving & Osler, 1968; Tulving & Pearlstone, 1966).

Results regarding the various personal characteristics examined in this study lead to some mixed results. For instance, subject expertise emerged as a significant predictor of KSD in both study one and study two. However, subject expertise led to a decrease in definitional knowledge. A potential explanation posed for this latter finding was that those with high subject expertise may have skimmed content they thought they already knew, thereby inadvertently missing important information.

Web expertise did not emerge as a significant predictor of knowledge in either study one or study two. However, in the basic correlation analyses of both studies, web expertise was related to Internet self-efficacy, thereby indicating a consistent relationship between the two concepts. With this relationship in mind, it should not be surprising to note that Internet self-efficacy also did not emerge as a significant predictor of knowledge in either study one or study two.

Motivation interacted with site design in study one to affect KSD. Specifically, highly motivated users of the relational site acquired denser knowledge structures, whereas highly motivated users of the definitional site acquired less dense structural knowledge. It appears as though the definitional site hindered KSD acquisition for those who were highly motivated while the relational site fostered such knowledge acquisition. This indicates that the highly motivated users of the definitional site focused intently on the definitions, thereby missing concept relationships. Motivation did not emerge as a significant predictor of KSD in study two.

Cognitive load (misunderstanding) interacted with site design in study one to predict definitional knowledge. Specifically, for those using the relational site condition, high CLM resulted in low definitional knowledge scores, medium CLM resulted in moderate definitional knowledge scores, and low CLM resulted in high definitional knowledge scores. Similarly, for those in the definitional site condition, high CLM resulted in low definitional knowledge scores (with no apparent differences in definitional knowledge for those experiencing moderate and low CLM). These findings appear to be consistent with cognitive load theory, suggesting the more difficulty someone experiences in understanding content and its structure, the less knowledge they will acquire. As for study two, CLE predicted denser knowledge structure, a finding that indicates that effort exerted and not necessarily cognitive load led to denser knowledge structure.

Results from these two studies provide some insight into definitional knowledge and knowledge structure, which were the primary foci of study one in that elaboration was manipulated and affected these two types of knowledge. Study two added further information to KSD issues and support for some of the findings in study one. What is lacking in this research are solid details regarding factual knowledge. Except for the finding that the control site enhanced factual knowledge over the other two sites, no other meaningful results were obtained regarding factual knowledge. Further research focusing on factual knowledge is certainly warranted based on the lack of significant findings from study one.

# Appendix A

## Study One Instructions

### Study Instructions

Please spend the next 20–30 minutes examining the website indicated below. It is important that you actively read through the site and focus on the information presented here. After viewing the website you will be given a brief quiz. Please do not try to memorize what you read, just try to understand the information presented. Please continue reading through the site until I tell you to stop.

http://www.jcomm.ohio-state.edu/jcortese/AltMedSite/index.htm

Alternate website addresses for the other two conditions:

http://www.jcomm.ohio-state.edu/jcortese/AltMedSite_d/index.htm
http://www.jcomm.ohio-state.edu/jcortese/AltMedSite_r/index.htm

# APPENDIX B

# STUDY ONE QUESTIONNAIRE

## HYPERMEDIA INFORMATION ACQUISITION STUDY

*Pre-Questionnaire*

It is important that you answer every question as honestly as possible. Your participation is voluntary and your answers to all questions will be kept anonymous and confidential.

Q. First Subject ID
Please enter your subject ID _____

*Here are a Few Questions about your use of the World Wide Web*

Q. Web Expertise 1
How many days out of the past week have you used the World Wide Web? (Use of the World Wide Web DOES NOT include checking email.)
_____ days (please give a single number, not a range)

Q. Web Expertise 2
Indicate your expertise in using the WWW (again, this DOES NOT include checking email) by clicking on the appropriate number.
- ☐  10—Expert
- ☐  9
- ☐  8
- ☐  7
- ☐  6
- ☐  5
- ☐  4

☐ 3
☐ 2
☐ 1—Novice

Q. Internet Self-Efficacy Scale

Items for this measure were adapted from existing self-efficacy (Eastin & LaRose, 2000; Joo, et al., 2000; Midgley, et al., 2000; Torkzadeh & van Dyke, 2001), expectancy outcome (LaRose, Mastro, & Eastin, 2001) and Internet use (Charney & Greenberg, 2002) measures.

Q. Subject Expertise

Please indicate your level of **expertise** regarding information about alternative medicine by clicking on the appropriate number from 1 to 10, where "10" indicates "expert" and "1" indicates "novice."

☐ 10—Expert
☐ 9
☐ 8
☐ 7
☐ 6
☐ 5
☐ 4
☐ 3
☐ 2
☐ 1—Novice

Finally, here are just a few last questions about you:

Q. Age

Please indicate your age as of your last birthday: _____

Q. Sex

Please click on the appropriate box to indicate if you are:
☐ Female
☐ Male

Q. Marital Status

Please click on the appropriate box to indicate if you are:

☐ Single (never married)

☐ Married

☐ Widowed

☐ Divorced

☐ Separated

Q. Class Standing

Please click on the appropriate box to indicate your current class standing:

☐ Freshman

☐ Sophomore

☐ Junior

☐ Senior

☐ Graduate Student

Q. Race

Please indicate the race you consider yourself by clicking on ALL that apply:

☐ Caucasian / White

☐ African–American

☐ Asian–American

☐ Hispanic

☐ Other _____

Q. Income

Please click on the appropriate box to indicate your estimated family income:

☐ under $10,000

☐ $10,000–$19,000

☐ $20,000–$29,000

☐ $30,000–$39,000

☐ $40,000–$49,000

☐   $50,000–$59,000
☐   $60,000–$69,000
☐   $70,000–$80,000
☐   over $80,000

## HYPERMEDIA INFORMATION ACQUISITION QUESTIONNAIRE

*Post-Questionnaire*

Q. Second Subject ID
Please enter your subject ID here _____

Q. Def. Manip. Check
While using the website, how much did you pay attention to the <u>definition</u> of each hyperlinked concept (as indicated by hyperlinked text)?
☐   10—Very close attention
☐   9
☐   8
☐   7
☐   6
☐   5
☐   4
☐   3
☐   2
☐   1—No attention at all

Q. Rel. Manip. Check
While using the website, how much did you pay attention to how pages of information were <u>connected to</u> other pages of information as indicated by the relationships specified by hyperlinked concepts?
☐   10—Very close attention
☐   9
☐   8

☐  7

☐  6

☐  5

☐  4

☐  3

☐  2

☐  1—No attention at all

Q. Cognitive Load (see Paas, 1992; Paas, et al., 1994)

Q. Cognitive Load Table (see Eveland & Dunwoody, 2001; Kalyuga, et al., 2001)

Q. Motivation (see Guay, et al., 2000)

*Knowledge Structure*

Next, please indicate the level of relatedness between the topic pairs presented. For each pair you are asked to indicate the extent to which you think they are related (or not related) by clicking on the appropriate choice: "very closely related," "closely related," "moderately related," "weakly related", or "unrelated."

Q. KSD1
Herbal Remedies and Homeopathy
☐   Very closely related
☐   Closely related
☐   Moderately related
☐   Weakly related
☐   Unrelated

Q. KSD2—Herbal Remedies and Vitamins
Q. KSD3—Herbal Remedies and Vegetarianism
Q. KSD4—Herbal Remedies and Raw Foodism
Q. KSD5—Herbal Remedies and Macrobiotics
Q. KSD6—Herbal Remedies and Fasting

Q. KSD7—Herbal Remedies and Weekend Monodiets

Q. KSD8—Herbal Remedies and Colon Therapy

Q. KSD9—Herbal Remedies and Chelation Therapy

Q. KSD10—Herbal Remedies and Acupuncture

Q. KSD11—Herbal Remedies and Acupressure

Q. KSD12—Herbal Remedies and Massage

Q. KSD13—Herbal Remedies and Reflexology

Q. KSD14—Herbal Remedies and Chiropractic

Q. KSD15—Herbal Remedies and Aromatherapy

Q. KSD16—Herbal Remedies and Meditation

Q. KSD17—Herbal Remedies and Qigong

Q. KSD18—Herbal Remedies and Yoga

Q. KSD19—Herbal Remedies and Tai Chi

Q. KSD20—Homeopathy and Vitamins

Q. KSD21—Homeopathy and Vegetarianism

Q. KSD22—Homeopathy and Raw Foodism

Q. KSD23—Homeopathy and Macrobiotics

Q. KSD24—Homeopathy and Fasting

Q. KSD25—Homeopathy and Weekend Monodiets

Q. KSD26—Homeopathy and Colon Therapy

Q. KSD27—Homeopathy and Chelation Therapy

Q. KSD28—Homeopathy and Acupuncture

Q. KSD29—Homeopathy and Acupressure

Q. KSD30—Homeopathy and Massage

Q. KSD31—Homeopathy and Reflexology

Q. KSD32—Homeopathy and Chiropractic

Q. KSD33—Homeopathy and Aromatherapy

Q. KSD34—Homeopathy and Meditation

Q. KSD35—Homeopathy and Qigong

Q. KSD36—Homeopathy and Yoga

Q. KSD37—Homeopathy and Tai Chi

Q. KSD38—Vitamins and Vegetarianism

Q. KSD39—Vitamins and Raw Foodism

Q. KSD40—Vitamins and Macrobiotics

Q. KSD41—Vitamins and Fasting

Q. KSD42—Vitamins and Weekend Monodiets

Q. KSD43—Vitamins and Colon Therapy

Q. KSD44—Vitamins and Chelation Therapy

Q. KSD45—Vitamins and Acupuncture

Q. KSD46—Vitamins and Acupressure

Q. KSD47—Vitamins and Massage

Q. KSD48—Vitamins and Reflexology

Q. KSD49—Vitamins and Chiropractic

Q. KSD50—Vitamins and Aromatherapy

Q. KSD51—Vitamins and Meditation

Q. KSD52—Vitamins and Qigong

Q. KSD53—Vitamins and Yoga

Q. KSD54—Vitamins and Tai Chi

Q. KSD55—Vegetarianism and Raw Foodism

Q. KSD56—Vegetarianism and Macrobiotics

Q. KSD57—Vegetarianism and Fasting

Q. KSD58—Vegetarianism and Weekend Monodiets

Q. KSD59—Vegetarianism and Colon Therapy

Q. KSD60—Vegetarianism and Chelation Therapy

Q. KSD61—Vegetarianism and Acupuncture

Q. KSD62—Vegetarianism and Acupressure

Q. KSD63—Vegetarianism and Massage

Q. KSD64—Vegetarianism and Reflexology

Q. KSD65—Vegetarianism and Chiropractic

Q. KSD66—Vegetarianism and Aromatherapy

Q. KSD67—Vegetarianism and Meditation

Q. KSD68—Vegetarianism and Qigong

Q. KSD69—Vegetarianism and Yoga

Q. KSD70—Vegetarianism and Tai Chi

Q. KSD71—Raw Foodism and Macrobiotics

Q. KSD72—Raw Foodism and Fasting

Q. KSD73—Raw Foodism and Weekend Monodiets

Q. KSD74—Raw Foodism and Colon Therapy

Q. KSD75—Raw Foodism and Chelation Therapy

Q. KSD76—Raw Foodism and Acupuncture

Q. KSD77—Raw Foodism and Acupressure

Q. KSD78—Raw Foodism and Massage

Q. KSD79—Raw Foodism and Reflexology

Q. KSD80—Raw Foodism and Chiropractic

Q. KSD81—Raw Foodism and Aromatherapy

Q. KSD82—Raw Foodism and Meditation

Q. KSD83—Raw Foodism and Qigong

Q. KSD84—Raw Foodism and Yoga

Q. KSD85—Raw Foodism and Tai Chi

Q. KSD86—Macrobiotics and Fasting

Q. KSD87—Macrobiotics and Weekend Monodiets

Q. KSD88—Macrobiotics and Colon Therapy

Q. KSD89—Macrobiotics and Chelation Therapy

Q. KSD90—Macrobiotics and Acupuncture

Q. KSD91—Macrobiotics and Acupressure

Q. KSD92—Macrobiotics and Massage

Q. KSD93—Macrobiotics and Reflexology

Q. KSD94—Macrobiotics and Chiropractic

Q. KSD95—Macrobiotics and Aromatherapy

Q. KSD96—Macrobiotics and Meditation

Q. KSD97—Macrobiotics and Qigong

Q. KSD98—Macrobiotics and Yoga

Q. KSD99—Macrobiotics and Tai Chi

Q. KSD100—Fasting and Weekend Monodiets

Q. KSD101—Fasting and Colon Therapy

Q. KSD102—Fasting and Chelation Therapy

Q. KSD103—Fasting and Acupuncture

Q. KSD104—Fasting and Acupressure

Q. KSD105—Fasting and Massage

Q. KSD106—Fasting and Reflexology

Q. KSD107—Fasting and Chiropractic

Q. KSD108—Fasting and Aromatherapy

Q. KSD109—Fasting and Meditation

Q. KSD110—Fasting and Qigong

Q. KSD111—Fasting and Yoga

Q. KSD112—Fasting and Tai Chi

Q. KSD113—Weekend Monodiets and Colon Therapy

Q. KSD114—Weekend Monodiets and Chelation Therapy

Q. KSD115—Weekend Monodiets and Acupuncture

Q. KSD116—Weekend Monodiets and Acupressure

Q. KSD117—Weekend Monodiets and Massage

Q. KSD118—Weekend Monodiets and Reflexology

Q. KSD119—Weekend Monodiets and Chiropractic

Q. KSD120—Weekend Monodiets and Aromatherapy

Q. KSD121—Weekend Monodiets and Meditation

Q. KSD122—Weekend Monodiets and Qigong

Q. KSD123—Weekend Monodiets and Yoga

Q. KSD124—Weekend Monodiets and Tai Chi

Q. KSD125—Colon Therapy and Chelation Therapy

Q. KSD126—Colon Therapy and Acupuncture

Q. KSD127—Colon Therapy and Acupressure

Q. KSD128—Colon Therapy and Massage

Q. KSD129—Colon Therapy and Reflexology

Q. KSD130—Colon Therapy and Chiropractic

Q. KSD131—Colon Therapy and Aromatherapy

Q. KSD132—Colon Therapy and Meditation

Q. KSD133—Colon Therapy and Qigong

Q. KSD134—Colon Therapy and Yoga

Q. KSD135—Colon Therapy and Tai Chi

Q. KSD136—Chelation Therapy and Acupuncture

Q. KSD137—Chelation Therapy and Acupressure

Q. KSD138—Chelation Therapy and Massage

Q. KSD139—Chelation Therapy and Reflexology

Q. KSD140—Chelation Therapy and Chiropractic

Q. KSD141—Chelation Therapy and Aromatherapy

Q. KSD142—Chelation Therapy and Meditation

Q. KSD143—Chelation Therapy and Qigong

Q. KSD144—Chelation Therapy and Yoga

Q. KSD145—Chelation Therapy and Tai Chi

Q. KSD146—Acupuncture and Acupressure

Q. KSD147—Acupuncture and Massage

Q. KSD148—Acupuncture and Reflexology

Q. KSD149—Acupuncture and Chiropractic

Q. KSD150—Acupuncture and Aromatherapy

Q. KSD151—Acupuncture and Meditation

Q. KSD152—Acupuncture and Qigong

Q. KSD153—Acupuncture and Yoga

Q. KSD154—Acupuncture and Tai Chi

Q. KSD155—Acupressure and Massage

Q. KSD156—Acupressure and Reflexology

Q. KSD157—Acupressure and Chiropractic

Q. KSD158—Acupressure and Aromatherapy

Q. KSD159—Acupressure and Meditation

Q. KSD160—Acupressure and Qigong

Q. KSD161—Acupressure and Yoga

Q. KSD162—Acupressure and Tai Chi

Q. KSD163—Massage and Reflexology

Q. KSD164—Massage and Chiropractic

Q. KSD165—Massage and Aromatherapy

Q. KSD166—Massage and Meditation

Q. KSD167—Massage and Qigong

Q. KSD168—Massage and Yoga

Q. KSD169—Massage and Tai Chi

Q. KSD170—Reflexology and Chiropractic

Q. KSD171—Reflexology and Aromatherapy

Q. KSD172—Reflexology and Meditation

Q. KSD173—Reflexology and Qigong

Q. KSD174—Reflexology and Yoga

Q. KSD175—Reflexology and Tai Chi

Q. KSD176—Chiropractic and Aromatherapy

Q. KSD177—Chiropractic and Meditation

Q. KSD178—Chiropractic and Qigong

Q. KSD179—Chiropractic and Yoga

Q. KSD180—Chiropractic and Tai Chi

Q. KSD181—Aromatherapy and Meditation

Q. KSD182—Aromatherapy and Qigong

Q. KSD183—Aromatherapy and Yoga

Q. KSD184—Aromatherapy and Tai Chi

Q. KSD185—Meditation and Qigong

Q. KSD186—Meditation and Yoga

Q. KSD187—Meditation and Tai Chi

Q. KSD188—Qigong and Yoga

Q. KSD189—Qigong and Tai Chi

Q. KSD190—Yoga and Tai Chi

The following questions are in the form of multiple choice and true / false questions. Please choose the best answer for each question by clicking on the corresponding button. (*Italics represent the answer.*)

1. CAM stands for:

☐ Chelation and Massage

☐ *Complementary and Alternative Medicine*

☐ Caloric Arterial Metabolism
☐ Conscious Asana Meditation

2. Although widely used by the American public, there are no governmental guidelines defining what constitutes a dietary supplement.
☐ True
☐ *False*

3. Which of the following statements about herbal supplements is **NOT** correct:
☐ It's important to know that just because an herbal supplement is labeled "natural" does not mean it is safe or without any harmful effects.
☐ Herbal supplements can act in the same way as drugs.
☐ If you use herbal supplements, it is best to do so under the guidance of a medical professional who has been properly trained in herbal medicine.
☐ *Herbal supplements are regulated by the U.S. Food and Drug Administration as medications.*

4. Which of the following is not a principle of homeopathy:
☐ Like cures like (Law of Similars)
☐ The more a remedy is diluted, the greater its potency (Law of the Infinitesimal Dose)
☐ An illness is specific to the individual (a holistic medical model)
☐ *Potency is increased when the remedy is administered under the individual's tongue (Law of Absorption)*

5. Four of the thirteen essential vitamins are fat-soluble, meaning that excess amounts are absorbed by body fat and stored for later use in case the body runs short of them in the future. These four vitamins are:
☐ A, C, D, E
☐ *A, D, E, K*

☐   A, B12, C, E
☐   A, B12, C, K

6. What percentage of U.S. adults eat the recommended servings of fruits and vegetables each day as detailed by the Food Guide Pyramid and the Dietary Guidelines for Americans?
☐   10%
☐   *25%*
☐   45%
☐   60%

7. Lacto ovo vegetarians:
☐   Do not eat milk and eggs
☐   *Do not eat meat, fish and poultry; but do eat milk and eggs*
☐   Eat only raw eggs and milk as their sources of protein
☐   None of the above

8. Raw foodists prefer eating food that has not been cooked over 116 degrees F because cooking food above this temperature:
☐   *Kills the nutrients and enzymes in the foods*
☐   Makes the food harder to digest
☐   Kills good bacteria in the food that is necessary for intestinal health
☐   Is not environmentally friendly, thereby creating bad karma that can be ingested with the food

9. A macrobiotic diet is mainly vegetarian, excluding all meat products except:
☐   Poultry
☐   Eggs
☐   *Seafood*
☐   Pork

10. Considering all parts of the human body, there are ??? sites of toxic accumulation?
☐  4
☐  *13*
☐  21
☐  32

11. The primary type of juice used in a juice fast is:
☐  *Vegetable*
☐  Fruit
☐  An equal mix of both vegetable and fruit

12. If you chose to participate in a weekend monodiet for detoxification, which food would be the best choice if you are experiencing digestive problems:
☐  Grapes
☐  Apples
☐  Pears
☐  *Papaya*

13. The function of colonic irrigation is to draw toxins from the blood and lymph system back into the colon for excretion.
☐  *True*
☐  False

14. EDTA (ethylenediaminetetraacetic acid) is a synthetic amino acid administered intravenously to aid detoxification using which of the following therapies:
☐  Metabolic Therapy
☐  *Chelation Therapy*
☐  Colon Therapy
☐  Alkaline Detoxification Diet Therapy

15. Which of the following statements about bodywork techniques are true?

☐    Bodywork is a mind-body medicine

☐    Bodywork therapies can be considered invasive

☐    *Bodywork therapies are more focused on enhancing well-being than on healing illness*

☐    All of the above

☐    None of the above

16. According to acupuncture theory, qi circulates in the body along twelve major energy pathways, called ???, each linked to specific internal organs and organ systems.

☐    Qigong Lines

☐    Veins

☐    *Meridians*

☐    Lymph Systems

17. Acupressure is just like acupuncture except that a trained practitioner puts gentle pressure on the hair-thin needles once they are inserted just under the patient's skin.

☐    True

☐    *False*

18. A hot rock message incorporates the use of a large basin containing intensely heated rocks. At the beginning of the massage session, water is poured over the rocks creating a steam rich in minerals contained in the rocks.

☐    True

☐    *False*

19. In reflexology, applying pressure to a reflex point on the ??? affects the corresponding body organ area.

☐    Head

☐    Ear

☐ Hand
☐ *Foot*

20. ??? may be the most commonly used alternative therapy in the United States today, with an estimated 50,000 professionals in this field, the third-largest group of health practitioners in the country.
☐ *Chiropractic*
☐ Acupuncture
☐ Herbal Remedies
☐ Massage

21. Relaxation is <u>directly</u> related to:
☐ Hypertension
☐ Cholesterol Levels
☐ *Stress*
☐ Heart Disease

22. Aromatherapy is a unique branch of herbal medicine that utilizes the medicinal properties found in:
☐ Flower Oils
☐ *Essential Oils*
☐ Herbal Oils
☐ Precious Oils

23. During the most basic form of concentrative meditation, one must be aware of and focused on their:
☐ *Breathing*
☐ Body
☐ Past memories
☐ Specific health issue of concern

24. What is the main purpose for qigong?
☐ It relaxes the individual
☐ *It enhances the flow of vital energy in the body*

☐   It helps the individual to achieve and maintain an optimal meditative state

☐   It stimulates the brain to release endorphins which aid in the healing process

25. Although exercising can be beneficial to the immune system, over exercising can weaken your immune system and make you sick.

☐   *True*

☐   False

26. Which one of these is not a Hatha Yoga position?

☐   Cobra

☐   Child's Pose

☐   Locust

☐   *Still Water*

27. Tai Chi is a more physically active form of: (*Not specifically noted in text = Bad question – left out of analysis.*)

☐   *Qigong*

☐   Yoga

☐   Reflexology

☐   Meditation

   The next several questions are definitions of alternative medicine terms. For each statement, choose the term it is defining from the list provided. The term to be defined is indicated by "XXXXXXX" in each statement. (Note: The choices are the same for each question.) (*Answer numbers are provided at the end of each question.*)

Q. DK1

XXXXXXX is the process of applying pressure to areas in the foot to alleviate problems within the body corresponding to the area of the foot where pressure is applied—17

1. Acupressure

2. Acupuncture

3. Alkaline-Detoxification Diets

4. Aromatherapy

5. Chelation therapy

6. Chiropractic

7. Colon therapies

8. Fasting

9. Herbal remedies

10. Homeopathy

11. Macrobiotics diets

12. Massage

13. Meditation

14. Metabolic therapies

15. QiGong

16. Raw food diets

17. Reflexology

18. Rolfing

19. Tai chi

20. Vegetarian diets

21. Vitamins

22. Weekend Monodiets

23. Yoga

Q. DK2

<u>XXXXXXX</u> draw toxins from the body and cleanses them through irrigation of the large intestine—7

Q. DK3

<u>XXXXXXX</u> enhances the flow of vital energy in the body (qi) through movement and breathing—15

Q. DK4

<u>XXXXXXX</u> come from animal or plant foods and supply the body with essential nutrients to convert food to energy and to help the body manufacture hormones, blood cells, and nervous system chemicals—21

Q. DK5

XXXXXXX focuses on the flow qi in the body through the use of movement reflecting opposing forces and balances—19

Q. DK6

XXXXXXX is administered by pressing a finger into acupoints on the body in order to alleviate pain or stress associated with each particular point—1

Q. DK7

XXXXXXX focuses attention on the breath, images, thoughts, or other sensations in order to balance physical, emotional, and mental states of an individual—13

Q. DK8

XXXXXXX include seafood; but not meat, poultry, eggs, dairy, certain vegetables (potato, pepper, and eggplant), refined sugar and tropical fruits—11

Q. DK9

XXXXXXX medicine is the practice of manipulating the spine to correct medical problems—6

Q. DK10

XXXXXXX uses tiny needles to alleviate pain and increase the immune response by balancing the flow of life energy (qi) throughout the body—2

Q. DK11

XXXXXXX are vegetarian and do not include foods that are heated over 116 degrees F because that is the temperature at which enzymes in the food are destroyed—16

Q. DK12

XXXXXXX are cleansing diets consisting of the ingestion of just one food for a two-day period—22

Q. DK13

XXXXXXX uses medicinal compounds of plant extracts and minerals to stimulate the body's natural tendency to heal itself—10

Q. DK14

XXXXXXX is a modified cleansing diet consisting of only liquids, such as juice or water—8

Q. DK15

XXXXXXX detoxifies the blood using a synthetic amino acid that is administered intravenously and binds to toxic metals in the blood—5

Q. DK16

XXXXXXX utilizes essential oils extracted from plants and herbs to treat various heath concerns or problems—4

Q. DK17

XXXXXXX combines posture and breathing to reduce stress, lower blood pressure, regulate the heart rate, and alleviate many types of medical concerns—23

Q. DK18

XXXXXXX are medicinal blends of herbs (or botanicals) created by harnessing the scent, flavor, or therapeutic properties of plants or plant parts—9

Q. DK19

XXXXXXX do include meat, fish and poultry—20 (Bad question—left out of analysis.)

Q. DK20

XXXXXXX is the process of rubbing the muscles in order to improve circulation, increase blood flow, and bring fresh oxygen to body tissues—12

# Appendix C

# Study Two Instructions

## Website Condition

For the next part of the study I ask that you spend the next 20–30 minutes examining a website. It is important that you actively read through the site and focus on the information presented here. After viewing the website you will be given a brief quiz. Please do not try to memorize what you read, just try to understand the information presented. Please continue reading through the site until I tell you to stop.

Click on the "**Study**" icon (shortcut) on your computer desktop to access the site. Please begin now.

## Puzzle Condition

For the next part of the study I ask that you spend the next 20–30 minutes solving an online crossword puzzle. It is important that you do your best to solve this puzzle in the time allotted. If you solve the puzzle or get to a point where you cannot fill in any more of the puzzle, please go to the next puzzle and do your best with that one. Continue in this fashion until I tell you to stop.

Click on the "**Study**" icon (shortcut) on your computer desktop to access the puzzle. Please begin now by using the instructions below.

## How to Access the Puzzle Once you are on the Site

Click on the featured puzzle button. Then choose your skill level (either is fine). You can type your answers into any highlighted block. To change from "across" to "down" and vice versa, just click on the first letter of the word. There is a "help" tab on the puzzle if you need further assistance. To access another puzzle, click on the "previous date" link at the top of your current puzzle.

# APPENDIX D

# STUDY TWO QUESTIONNAIRE

## HYPERMEDIA INFORMATION ACQUISITION QUESTIONNAIRE

*Pre-Questionnaire*

It is important that you answer every question as honestly as possible. Your participation is voluntary and your answers to all questions will be kept anonymous and confidential.

Q. First Subject ID
Please enter your subject ID _____

Q. Web Expertise 2
Indicate your expertise in using the WWW (this DOES NOT include checking email) by clicking on the appropriate number.

☐   10—Expert
☐   9
☐   8
☐   7
☐   6
☐   5
☐   4
☐   3
☐   2
☐   1—Novice

Q. Internet Self Efficacy Scale
Items for this measure were adapted from existing self-efficacy (Eastin & LaRose, 2000; Joo, et al., 2000; Midgley, et al., 2000; Torkzadeh & van Dyke, 2001), expectancy outcome (LaRose, Mastro, & Eastin, 2001) and Internet use (Charney & Greenberg, 2002) measures.

Q. Subject Expertise

Please indicate your level of **expertise** regarding information about alternative medicine by clicking on the appropriate number from 1 to 10, where "10" indicates "expert" and "1" indicates "novice."

☐ 10—Expert
☐ 9
☐ 8
☐ 7
☐ 6
☐ 5
☐ 4
☐ 3
☐ 2
☐ 1—Novice

*Knowledge Structure*

Next, please indicate the level of relatedness between the topic pairs presented. For each pair you are asked to indicate the extent to which you think they are related (or not related) by clicking on the appropriate choice: "very closely related," "closely related," "moderately related," "weakly related", or "unrelated."

Q. KSD1
Herbal Remedies and Homeopathy
☐ Very closely related
☐ Closely related
☐ Moderately related
☐ Weakly related
☐ Unrelated

Q. KSD2—Herbal Remedies and Vitamins
Q. KSD3—Herbal Remedies and Vegetarianism
Q. KSD4—Herbal Remedies and Raw Foodism

Q. KSD5—Herbal Remedies and Macrobiotics

Q. KSD6—Herbal Remedies and Fasting

Q. KSD7—Herbal Remedies and Weekend Monodiets

Q. KSD8—Herbal Remedies and Colon Therapy

Q. KSD9—Herbal Remedies and Chelation Therapy

Q. KSD10—Herbal Remedies and Acupuncture

Q. KSD11—Herbal Remedies and Acupressure

Q. KSD12—Herbal Remedies and Massage

Q. KSD13—Herbal Remedies and Reflexology

Q. KSD14—Herbal Remedies and Chiropractic

Q. KSD15—Herbal Remedies and Aromatherapy

Q. KSD16—Herbal Remedies and Meditation

Q. KSD17—Herbal Remedies and Qigong

Q. KSD18—Herbal Remedies and Yoga

Q. KSD19—Herbal Remedies and Tai Chi

Q. KSD20—Homeopathy and Vitamins

Q. KSD21—Homeopathy and Vegetarianism

Q. KSD22—Homeopathy and Raw Foodism

Q. KSD23—Homeopathy and Macrobiotics

Q. KSD24—Homeopathy and Fasting

Q. KSD25—Homeopathy and Weekend Monodiets

Q. KSD26—Homeopathy and Colon Therapy

Q. KSD27—Homeopathy and Chelation Therapy

Q. KSD28—Homeopathy and Acupuncture

Q. KSD29—Homeopathy and Acupressure

Q. KSD30—Homeopathy and Massage

Q. KSD31—Homeopathy and Reflexology

Q. KSD32—Homeopathy and Chiropractic

Q. KSD33—Homeopathy and Aromatherapy

Q. KSD34—Homeopathy and Meditation

Q. KSD35—Homeopathy and Qigong

Q. KSD36—Homeopathy and Yoga

Q. KSD37—Homeopathy and Tai Chi
Q. KSD38—Vitamins and Vegetarianism
Q. KSD39—Vitamins and Raw Foodism
Q. KSD40—Vitamins and Macrobiotics
Q. KSD41—Vitamins and Fasting
Q. KSD42—Vitamins and Weekend Monodiets
Q. KSD43—Vitamins and Colon Therapy
Q. KSD44—Vitamins and Chelation Therapy
Q. KSD45—Vitamins and Acupuncture
Q. KSD46—Vitamins and Acupressure
Q. KSD47—Vitamins and Massage
Q. KSD48—Vitamins and Reflexology
Q. KSD49—Vitamins and Chiropractic
Q. KSD50—Vitamins and Aromatherapy
Q. KSD51—Vitamins and Meditation
Q. KSD52—Vitamins and Qigong
Q. KSD53—Vitamins and Yoga
Q. KSD54—Vitamins and Tai Chi
Q. KSD55—Vegetarianism and Raw Foodism
Q. KSD56—Vegetarianism and Macrobiotics
Q. KSD57—Vegetarianism and Fasting
Q. KSD58—Vegetarianism and Weekend Monodiets
Q. KSD59—Vegetarianism and Colon Therapy
Q. KSD60—Vegetarianism and Chelation Therapy
Q. KSD61—Vegetarianism and Acupuncture
Q. KSD62—Vegetarianism and Acupressure
Q. KSD63—Vegetarianism and Massage
Q. KSD64—Vegetarianism and Reflexology
Q. KSD65—Vegetarianism and Chiropractic
Q. KSD66—Vegetarianism and Aromatherapy
Q. KSD67—Vegetarianism and Meditation
Q. KSD68—Vegetarianism and Qigong

Q. KSD69—Vegetarianism and Yoga

Q. KSD70—Vegetarianism and Tai Chi

Q. KSD71—Raw Foodism and Macrobiotics

Q. KSD72—Raw Foodism and Fasting

Q. KSD73—Raw Foodism and Weekend Monodiets

Q. KSD74—Raw Foodism and Colon Therapy

Q. KSD75—Raw Foodism and Chelation Therapy

Q. KSD76—Raw Foodism and Acupuncture

Q. KSD77—Raw Foodism and Acupressure

Q. KSD78—Raw Foodism and Massage

Q. KSD79—Raw Foodism and Reflexology

Q. KSD80—Raw Foodism and Chiropractic

Q. KSD81—Raw Foodism and Aromatherapy

Q. KSD82—Raw Foodism and Meditation

Q. KSD83—Raw Foodism and Qigong

Q. KSD84—Raw Foodism and Yoga

Q. KSD85—Raw Foodism and Tai Chi

Q. KSD86—Macrobiotics and Fasting

Q. KSD87—Macrobiotics and Weekend Monodiets

Q. KSD88—Macrobiotics and Colon Therapy

Q. KSD89—Macrobiotics and Chelation Therapy

Q. KSD90—Macrobiotics and Acupuncture

Q. KSD91—Macrobiotics and Acupressure

Q. KSD92—Macrobiotics and Massage

Q. KSD93—Macrobiotics and Reflexology

Q. KSD94—Macrobiotics and Chiropractic

Q. KSD95—Macrobiotics and Aromatherapy

Q. KSD96—Macrobiotics and Meditation

Q. KSD97—Macrobiotics and Qigong

Q. KSD98—Macrobiotics and Yoga

Q. KSD99—Macrobiotics and Tai Chi

Q. KSD100—Fasting and Weekend Monodiets

Q. KSD101—Fasting and Colon Therapy
Q. KSD102—Fasting and Chelation Therapy
Q. KSD103—Fasting and Acupuncture
Q. KSD104—Fasting and Acupressure
Q. KSD105—Fasting and Massage
Q. KSD106—Fasting and Reflexology
Q. KSD107—Fasting and Chiropractic
Q. KSD108—Fasting and Aromatherapy
Q. KSD109—Fasting and Meditation
Q. KSD110—Fasting and Qigong
Q. KSD111—Fasting and Yoga
Q. KSD112—Fasting and Tai Chi
Q. KSD113—Weekend Monodiets and Colon Therapy
Q. KSD114—Weekend Monodiets and Chelation Therapy
Q. KSD115—Weekend Monodiets and Acupuncture
Q. KSD116—Weekend Monodiets and Acupressure
Q. KSD117—Weekend Monodiets and Massage
Q. KSD118—Weekend Monodiets and Reflexology
Q. KSD119—Weekend Monodiets and Chiropractic
Q. KSD120—Weekend Monodiets and Aromatherapy
Q. KSD121—Weekend Monodiets and Meditation
Q. KSD122—Weekend Monodiets and Qigong
Q. KSD123—Weekend Monodiets and Yoga
Q. KSD124—Weekend Monodiets and Tai Chi
Q. KSD125—Colon Therapy and Chelation Therapy
Q. KSD126—Colon Therapy and Acupuncture
Q. KSD127—Colon Therapy and Acupressure
Q. KSD128—Colon Therapy and Massage
Q. KSD129—Colon Therapy and Reflexology
Q. KSD130—Colon Therapy and Chiropractic
Q. KSD131—Colon Therapy and Aromatherapy
Q. KSD132—Colon Therapy and Meditation

Q. KSD133—Colon Therapy and Qigong

Q. KSD134—Colon Therapy and Yoga

Q. KSD135—Colon Therapy and Tai Chi

Q. KSD136—Chelation Therapy and Acupuncture

Q. KSD137—Chelation Therapy and Acupressure

Q. KSD138—Chelation Therapy and Massage

Q. KSD139—Chelation Therapy and Reflexology

Q. KSD140—Chelation Therapy and Chiropractic

Q. KSD141—Chelation Therapy and Aromatherapy

Q. KSD142—Chelation Therapy and Meditation

Q. KSD143—Chelation Therapy and Qigong

Q. KSD144—Chelation Therapy and Yoga

Q. KSD145—Chelation Therapy and Tai Chi

Q. KSD146—Acupuncture and Acupressure

Q. KSD147—Acupuncture and Massage

Q. KSD148—Acupuncture and Reflexology

Q. KSD149—Acupuncture and Chiropractic

Q. KSD150—Acupuncture and Aromatherapy

Q. KSD151—Acupuncture and Meditation

Q. KSD152—Acupuncture and Qigong

Q. KSD153—Acupuncture and Yoga

Q. KSD154—Acupuncture and Tai Chi

Q. KSD155—Acupressure and Massage

Q. KSD156—Acupressure and Reflexology

Q. KSD157—Acupressure and Chiropractic

Q. KSD158—Acupressure and Aromatherapy

Q. KSD159—Acupressure and Meditation

Q. KSD160—Acupressure and Qigong

Q. KSD161—Acupressure and Yoga

Q. KSD162—Acupressure and Tai Chi

Q. KSD163—Massage and Reflexology

Q. KSD164—Massage and Chiropractic

Q. KSD165—Massage and Aromatherapy

Q. KSD166—Massage and Meditation

Q. KSD167—Massage and Qigong

Q. KSD168—Massage and Yoga

Q. KSD169—Massage and Tai Chi

Q. KSD170—Reflexology and Chiropractic

Q. KSD171—Reflexology and Aromatherapy

Q. KSD172—Reflexology and Meditation

Q. KSD173—Reflexology and Qigong

Q. KSD174—Reflexology and Yoga

Q. KSD175—Reflexology and Tai Chi

Q. KSD176—Chiropractic and Aromatherapy

Q. KSD177—Chiropractic and Meditation

Q. KSD178—Chiropractic and Qigong

Q. KSD179—Chiropractic and Yoga

Q. KSD180—Chiropractic and Tai Chi

Q. KSD181—Aromatherapy and Meditation

Q. KSD182—Aromatherapy and Qigong

Q. KSD183—Aromatherapy and Yoga

Q. KSD184—Aromatherapy and Tai Chi

Q. KSD185—Meditation and Qigong

Q. KSD186—Meditation and Yoga

Q. KSD187—Meditation and Tai Chi

Q. KSD188—Qigong and Yoga

Q. KSD189—Qigong and Tai Chi

Q. KSD190—Yoga and Tai Chi

## DISTRACTOR QUESTIONS STARTS HERE ... (55 QUESTIONS)

Q. KSD191—Heart Disease and High Blood Pressure

Q. KSD192—Heart Disease and Obesity

Q. KSD193—Heart Disease and Chronic Pain

Q. KSD194—Heart Disease and Allergies

Q. KSD195—Heart Disease and Emphysema

Q. KSD196—Heart Disease and Smoking

Q. KSD197—Heart Disease and Drinking Alcohol

Q. KSD198—Heart Disease and Exercise

Q. KSD199—Heart Disease and Stress

Q. KSD200—Heart Disease and Nutrition

Q. KSD201—High Blood Pressure and Obesity

Q. KSD202—High Blood Pressure and Chronic Pain

Q. KSD203—High Blood Pressure and Allergies

Q. KSD204—High Blood Pressure and Emphysema

Q. KSD205—High Blood Pressure and Smoking

Q. KSD206—High Blood Pressure and Drinking Alcohol

Q. KSD207—High Blood Pressure and Exercise

Q. KSD208—High Blood Pressure and Stress

Q. KSD209—High Blood Pressure and Nutrition

Q. KSD210—Obesity and Chronic Pain

Q. KSD211—Obesity and Allergies

Q. KSD212—Obesity and Emphysema

Q. KSD213—Obesity and Smoking

Q. KSD214—Obesity and Drinking Alcohol

Q. KSD215—Obesity and Exercise

Q. KSD216—Obesity and Stress

Q. KSD217—Obesity and Nutrition

Q. KSD218—Chronic Pain and Allergies

Q. KSD219—Chronic Pain and Emphysema

Q. KSD220—Chronic Pain and Smoking

Q. KSD221—Chronic Pain and Drinking Alcohol

Q. KSD222—Chronic Pain and Exercise

Q. KSD223—Chronic Pain and Stress

Q. KSD224—Chronic Pain and Nutrition

Q. KSD225—Allergies and Emphysema

Q. KSD226—Allergies and Smoking

Q. KSD227—Allergies and Drinking Alcohol

Q. KSD228—Allergies and Exercise

Q. KSD229—Allergies and Stress

Q. KSD230—Allergies and Nutrition

Q. KSD231—Emphysema and Smoking

Q. KSD232—Emphysema and Drinking Alcohol

Q. KSD233—Emphysema and Exercise

Q. KSD234—Emphysema and Stress

Q. KSD235—Emphysema and Nutrition

Q. KSD236—Smoking and Drinking Alcohol

Q. KSD237—Smoking and Exercise

Q. KSD238—Smoking and Stress

Q. KSD239—Smoking and Nutrition

Q. KSD240—Drinking Alcohol and Exercise

Q. KSD241—Drinking Alcohol and Stress

Q. KSD242—Drinking Alcohol and Nutrition

Q. KSD243—Exercise and Stress

Q. KSD244—Exercise and Nutrition

Q. KSD245—Stress and Nutrition

Finally, here are just a few last questions about you:

Q. Age
Please indicate your age as of your last birthday: _____

Q. Sex
Please click on the appropriate box to indicate if you are:
☐  Female
☐  Male

Q. Marital Status

Please click on the appropriate box to indicate if you are:

☐   Single (never married)

☐   Married

☐   Widowed

☐   Divorced

☐   Separated

Q. Class Standing

Please click on the appropriate box to indicate your current class standing:

☐   Freshman

☐   Sophomore

☐   Junior

☐   Senior

☐   Graduate Student

Q. Race

Please indicate the race you consider yourself by clicking on ALL that apply:

☐   Caucasian / White

☐   African–American

☐   Asian–American

☐   Hispanic

☐   Other _____

Q. Income

Please click on the appropriate box to indicate your estimated family income:

☐   under $10,000

☐   $10,000–$19,000

☐   $20,000–$29,000

☐   $30,000–$39,000

☐   $40,000–$49,000

☐   $50,000–$59,000
☐   $60,000–$69,000
☐   $70,000–$80,000
☐   over $80,000

## HYPERMEDIA INFORMATION ACQUISITION QUESTIONNAIRE

*Post Questionnaire*

Q. Second Subject ID
Please enter your subject ID here _____

Q. Cognitive Load (see Paas, 1992; Paas, et al., 1994)

Q. Motivation (see Guay, et al., 2000)

*Knowledge Structure*

Next, please indicate the level of relatedness between the topic pairs presented. For each pair you are asked to indicate the extent to which you think they are related (or not related) by clicking on the appropriate choice: "very closely related," "closely related," "moderately related," "weakly related", or "unrelated."

Q. KSD1
Herbal Remedies and Homeopathy
☐   Very closely related
☐   Closely related
☐   Moderately related
☐   Weakly related
☐   Unrelated

Q. KSD2—Herbal Remedies and Vitamins
Q. KSD3—Herbal Remedies and Vegetarianism
Q. KSD4—Herbal Remedies and Raw Foodism

Q. KSD5—Herbal Remedies and Macrobiotics

Q. KSD6—Herbal Remedies and Fasting

Q. KSD7—Herbal Remedies and Weekend Monodiets

Q. KSD8—Herbal Remedies and Colon Therapy

Q. KSD9—Herbal Remedies and Chelation Therapy

Q. KSD10—Herbal Remedies and Acupuncture

Q. KSD11—Herbal Remedies and Acupressure

Q. KSD12—Herbal Remedies and Massage

Q. KSD13—Herbal Remedies and Reflexology

Q. KSD14—Herbal Remedies and Chiropractic

Q. KSD15—Herbal Remedies and Aromatherapy

Q. KSD16—Herbal Remedies and Meditation

Q. KSD17—Herbal Remedies and Qigong

Q. KSD18—Herbal Remedies and Yoga

Q. KSD19—Herbal Remedies and Tai Chi

Q. KSD20—Homeopathy and Vitamins

Q. KSD21—Homeopathy and Vegetarianism

Q. KSD22—Homeopathy and Raw Foodism

Q. KSD23—Homeopathy and Macrobiotics

Q. KSD24—Homeopathy and Fasting

Q. KSD25—Homeopathy and Weekend Monodiets

Q. KSD26—Homeopathy and Colon Therapy

Q. KSD27—Homeopathy and Chelation Therapy

Q. KSD28—Homeopathy and Acupuncture

Q. KSD29—Homeopathy and Acupressure

Q. KSD30—Homeopathy and Massage

Q. KSD31—Homeopathy and Reflexology

Q. KSD32—Homeopathy and Chiropractic

Q. KSD33—Homeopathy and Aromatherapy

Q. KSD34—Homeopathy and Meditation

Q. KSD35—Homeopathy and Qigong

Q. KSD36—Homeopathy and Yoga

Q. KSD37—Homeopathy and Tai Chi

Q. KSD38—Vitamins and Vegetarianism

Q. KSD39—Vitamins and Raw Foodism

Q. KSD40—Vitamins and Macrobiotics

Q. KSD41—Vitamins and Fasting

Q. KSD42—Vitamins and Weekend Monodiets

Q. KSD43—Vitamins and Colon Therapy

Q. KSD44—Vitamins and Chelation Therapy

Q. KSD45—Vitamins and Acupuncture

Q. KSD46—Vitamins and Acupressure

Q. KSD47—Vitamins and Massage

Q. KSD48—Vitamins and Reflexology

Q. KSD49—Vitamins and Chiropractic

Q. KSD50—Vitamins and Aromatherapy

Q. KSD51—Vitamins and Meditation

Q. KSD52—Vitamins and Qigong

Q. KSD53—Vitamins and Yoga

Q. KSD54—Vitamins and Tai Chi

Q. KSD55—Vegetarianism and Raw Foodism

Q. KSD56—Vegetarianism and Macrobiotics

Q. KSD57—Vegetarianism and Fasting

Q. KSD58—Vegetarianism and Weekend Monodiets

Q. KSD59—Vegetarianism and Colon Therapy

Q. KSD60—Vegetarianism and Chelation Therapy

Q. KSD61—Vegetarianism and Acupuncture

Q. KSD62—Vegetarianism and Acupressure

Q. KSD63—Vegetarianism and Massage

Q. KSD64—Vegetarianism and Reflexology

Q. KSD65—Vegetarianism and Chiropractic

Q. KSD66—Vegetarianism and Aromatherapy

Q. KSD67—Vegetarianism and Meditation

Q. KSD68—Vegetarianism and Qigong

Q. KSD69—Vegetarianism and Yoga

Q. KSD70—Vegetarianism and Tai Chi

Q. KSD71—Raw Foodism and Macrobiotics

Q. KSD72—Raw Foodism and Fasting

Q. KSD73—Raw Foodism and Weekend Monodiets

Q. KSD74—Raw Foodism and Colon Therapy

Q. KSD75—Raw Foodism and Chelation Therapy

Q. KSD76—Raw Foodism and Acupuncture

Q. KSD77—Raw Foodism and Acupressure

Q. KSD78—Raw Foodism and Massage

Q. KSD79—Raw Foodism and Reflexology

Q. KSD80—Raw Foodism and Chiropractic

Q. KSD81—Raw Foodism and Aromatherapy

Q. KSD82—Raw Foodism and Meditation

Q. KSD83—Raw Foodism and Qigong

Q. KSD84—Raw Foodism and Yoga

Q. KSD85—Raw Foodism and Tai Chi

Q. KSD86—Macrobiotics and Fasting

Q. KSD87—Macrobiotics and Weekend Monodiets

Q. KSD88—Macrobiotics and Colon Therapy

Q. KSD89—Macrobiotics and Chelation Therapy

Q. KSD90—Macrobiotics and Acupuncture

Q. KSD91—Macrobiotics and Acupressure

Q. KSD92—Macrobiotics and Massage

Q. KSD93—Macrobiotics and Reflexology

Q. KSD94—Macrobiotics and Chiropractic

Q. KSD95—Macrobiotics and Aromatherapy

Q. KSD96—Macrobiotics and Meditation

Q. KSD97—Macrobiotics and Qigong

Q. KSD98—Macrobiotics and Yoga

Q. KSD99—Macrobiotics and Tai Chi

Q. KSD100—Fasting and Weekend Monodiets

Q. KSD101—Fasting and Colon Therapy
Q. KSD102—Fasting and Chelation Therapy
Q. KSD103—Fasting and Acupuncture
Q. KSD104—Fasting and Acupressure
Q. KSD105—Fasting and Massage
Q. KSD106—Fasting and Reflexology
Q. KSD107—Fasting and Chiropractic
Q. KSD108—Fasting and Aromatherapy
Q. KSD109—Fasting and Meditation
Q. KSD110—Fasting and Qigong
Q. KSD111—Fasting and Yoga
Q. KSD112—Fasting and Tai Chi
Q. KSD113—Weekend Monodiets and Colon Therapy
Q. KSD114—Weekend Monodiets and Chelation Therapy
Q. KSD115—Weekend Monodiets and Acupuncture
Q. KSD116—Weekend Monodiets and Acupressure
Q. KSD117—Weekend Monodiets and Massage
Q. KSD118—Weekend Monodiets and Reflexology
Q. KSD119—Weekend Monodiets and Chiropractic
Q. KSD120—Weekend Monodiets and Aromatherapy
Q. KSD121—Weekend Monodiets and Meditation
Q. KSD122—Weekend Monodiets and Qigong
Q. KSD123—Weekend Monodiets and Yoga
Q. KSD124—Weekend Monodiets and Tai Chi
Q. KSD125—Colon Therapy and Chelation Therapy
Q. KSD126—Colon Therapy and Acupuncture
Q. KSD127—Colon Therapy and Acupressure
Q. KSD128—Colon Therapy and Massage
Q. KSD129—Colon Therapy and Reflexology
Q. KSD130—Colon Therapy and Chiropractic
Q. KSD131—Colon Therapy and Aromatherapy
Q. KSD132—Colon Therapy and Meditation

Q. KSD133—Colon Therapy and Qigong

Q. KSD134—Colon Therapy and Yoga

Q. KSD135—Colon Therapy and Tai Chi

Q. KSD136—Chelation Therapy and Acupuncture

Q. KSD137—Chelation Therapy and Acupressure

Q. KSD138—Chelation Therapy and Massage

Q. KSD139—Chelation Therapy and Reflexology

Q. KSD140—Chelation Therapy and Chiropractic

Q. KSD141—Chelation Therapy and Aromatherapy

Q. KSD142—Chelation Therapy and Meditation

Q. KSD143—Chelation Therapy and Qigong

Q. KSD144—Chelation Therapy and Yoga

Q. KSD145—Chelation Therapy and Tai Chi

Q. KSD146—Acupuncture and Acupressure

Q. KSD147—Acupuncture and Massage

Q. KSD148—Acupuncture and Reflexology

Q. KSD149—Acupuncture and Chiropractic

Q. KSD150—Acupuncture and Aromatherapy

Q. KSD151—Acupuncture and Meditation

Q. KSD152—Acupuncture and Qigong

Q. KSD153—Acupuncture and Yoga

Q. KSD154—Acupuncture and Tai Chi

Q. KSD155—Acupressure and Massage

Q. KSD156—Acupressure and Reflexology

Q. KSD157—Acupressure and Chiropractic

Q. KSD158—Acupressure and Aromatherapy

Q. KSD159—Acupressure and Meditation

Q. KSD160—Acupressure and Qigong

Q. KSD161—Acupressure and Yoga

Q. KSD162—Acupressure and Tai Chi

Q. KSD163—Massage and Reflexology

Q. KSD164—Massage and Chiropractic

Q. KSD165—Massage and Aromatherapy

Q. KSD166—Massage and Meditation

Q. KSD167—Massage and Qigong

Q. KSD168—Massage and Yoga

Q. KSD169—Massage and Tai Chi

Q. KSD170—Reflexology and Chiropractic

Q. KSD171—Reflexology and Aromatherapy

Q. KSD172—Reflexology and Meditation

Q. KSD173—Reflexology and Qigong

Q. KSD174—Reflexology and Yoga

Q. KSD175—Reflexology and Tai Chi

Q. KSD176—Chiropractic and Aromatherapy

Q. KSD177—Chiropractic and Meditation

Q. KSD178—Chiropractic and Qigong

Q. KSD179—Chiropractic and Yoga

Q. KSD180—Chiropractic and Tai Chi

Q. KSD181—Aromatherapy and Meditation

Q. KSD182—Aromatherapy and Qigong

Q. KSD183—Aromatherapy and Yoga

Q. KSD184—Aromatherapy and Tai Chi

Q. KSD185—Meditation and Qigong

Q. KSD186—Meditation and Yoga

Q. KSD187—Meditation and Tai Chi

Q. KSD188—Qigong and Yoga

Q. KSD189—Qigong and Tai Chi

Q. KSD190—Yoga and Tai Chi

# REFERENCES

Astleitner, H., & Leutner, D. (1996). Applying standard network analysis to hypermedia systems: Implications for learning. *Journal of Educational Computing Research, 14*, 285–303.

Atkinson, R. C., & Shiffrin, R. M. (1968). Human memory: A proposed system and its control processes. In K. W. Spence & J. T. Spence (Eds.), *The psychology of learning and motivation* (pp. 89–195). Academic Press: New York.

Bandura, A. (1986). *Social foundations of thought and action: A social cognitive theory*. New Jersey: Prentice-Hall.

———. (1999). Social cognitive theory of personality. In D. Cervone, & Y. Shoda (Eds.), *The coherence of personality: Social-cognitive bases of consistency, variability, and organization* (pp. 185–241). New York: Guilford Press.

———. (2001). Social cognitive theory: An agentic perspective. *Annual Review of Psychology, 52*, 1–26.

———. (2002a). Growing primacy of human agency in adaptation and change in the electronic era. *European Psychologist, 7*, 2–16.

———. (2002b). Social cognitive theory of mass communication. In J. Bryant, & D. Zillmann (Eds.), *Media effects: Advances in theory and research* (2nd ed.), (pp. 121–153). Mahwah, New Jersey: Erlbaum.

Bantz, C. R. (1982). Exploring uses and gratifications: A comparison of reported uses of television and reported uses of favorite program type. *Communication Research, 9*, 352–379.

Barab, S. A., Fajen, B. R., Kulikowich, J. M., & Young, M. F. (1996). Assessing hypermedia navigation through pathfinder: Prospects and limitations. *Journal of Educational Computing Research, 15*, 185–205.

Bieber, M. (2000). Hypertext. In A. Ralson, E. Reilly, & D. Hemmendinger (Eds.), *Encyclopedia of computer science* (4th ed.) (pp. 799–805). London: Nature Publishing Group.

Bieber, M., Vitali, F., Ashman, H., Balasubramanian, V., & Oinas-Kukkonen, H. (1997). Fourth generation hypermedia: Some missing links for the World Wide Web. *International Journal of Human-Computer Studies, 47*, 31–65.

Bong, M., & Hocevar, D. (2002). Measuring self-efficacy: Multitrait-multimethod comparison of scaling procedures. *Applied Measurement in Education, 15*, 143–171.

Brown, A. L. (1988). Motivation to learn and understand: On taking charge of one's own learning. *Cognition and Instruction, 5*, 311–321.

Calisir, F., & Gurel, Z. (2003). Influence of text structure and prior knowledge of the learner on reading comprehension, browsing and perceived control. *Computers in Human Behavior, 19*, 135–145.

Campbell, D., & Stanley, J. (1963). *Experimental and quasi-experimental designs for research.* Chicago: Rand McNally.

Carmel, E., Stephen, C., & Chen, H. (1992). Browsing in hypertext: A cognitive study. *IEEE Transactions on Systems, Man, and Cybernetics, 22*, 865–883.

Cassell, M. M., Jackson, C., & Cheuvront, B. (1998). Health communication on the Internet: An effective channel for health behavior change? *Journal of Health Communication, 3*, 71–79.

Charney, T., & Greenberg, B. S. (2002). Uses and gratifications of the Internet. In C. A. Lin & D. J. Atkin (Eds.), *Communication technology & society: Audience adoption and uses* (pp. 379–407). Cresskill, New Jersey: Hampton.

Chen, P., & McGrath, D. (2003). Moments of joy: Student engagement and conceptual learning in the design of hypermedia documents. *Journal of Research on Technology in Education, 35*, 402–422.

Clariana, R. B., & Lee, D. (2001). The effects of recognition and recall study tasks with feedback in a computer-based vocabulary lesson. *ETR & D: Educational Technology Research & Development, 49*(3), 23–36.

Cohen, J. (1965). Some statistical issues in psychological research. In B. B. Wolman (Ed.), *Handbook of clinical psychology* (pp. 95–121). New York: McGraw-Hill.

Craik, F. I. M., & Lockhart, R. S. (1972). Levels of processing: A framework for memory research. *Journal of Verbal Learning and Verbal Behavior, 11*, 671–684.

Cress, U., & Knabel, O. B. (2003). Previews in hypertexts: Effects on navigation and knowledge acquisition. *Journal of Computer Assisted Learning, 19*, 517–527.

Deci, E. L., & Ryan, R. M. (1985). *Intrinsic motivation and self-determination in human behavior.* New York: Plenum.

Deci, E. L., Vallerand, R. J., Pelletier, L. G., & Ryan, R. M. (1991). Motivation and education: The self-determination perspective. *Educational Psychologist, 26*, 325–346.

de Jong, T., & van der Hulst, A. (2002). The effects of graphical overviews on knowledge acquisition in hypertext. *Journal of Computer Assisted Learning, 18*, 219–231.

Eastin, M. S., & LaRose, R. (2000). Internet self-efficacy and the psychology of the digital divide. *Journal of Computer-Mediated Communication, 6*, 1–20.

Eisenberger, R., & Cameron, J. (1996). Detrimental effects of reward: Reality or myth? *American Psychologist, 51*, 1153–1166.

Entwistle, N., & Waterston, S. (1988). Approaches to studying and levels of processing in university students. *British Journal of Educational Psychology, 58*, 258–265.

Ertmer, P. A., & Newby, T. J. (1993). Behaviorism, cognitivism, constructivism: Comparing critical features from an instructional design perspective. *Performance Improvement Quarterly, 6*(4), 50–72.

Estes, W. K. (1999). Models of human memory: A 30-year retrospective. In C. Izawa (Ed.), *On human memory: Evolution, progress, and reflections on the 30th anniversary of the Atkinson–Shiffrin model* (pp. 59–86). New Jersey: Erlbaum.

Eveland, W. P., Jr., Cortese, J., Park, H., & Dunwoody, S. (2004). How web site organization influences free recall, factual knowledge, and knowledge structure. *Human Communication Research, 30*, 208–233.

Eveland, W. P., Jr., & Dunwoody, S. (1998). Users and navigation patterns of a science World Wide Web site for the public. *Public Understanding of Science, 7*, 285–311.

————. (2000). Examining information processing on the World Wide Web using think aloud protocols. *Media Psychology, 2*, 219–244.

————. (2001). User control and structural isomorphism or disorientation and cognitive load? Learning from the Web versus print. *Communication Research, 28*, 48–78.

Eveland, W. P., Jr., Marton, K., & Seo, M. (2004). Moving beyond "just the facts": The influence of online news on the content and structure of public affairs knowledge. *Communication Research, 30*, 1–27.

Eveland, W. P., Jr., Seo, M., & Marton, K. (2002). Learning from the news in campaign 2000: An experimental comparison of TV news, newspapers, and online news. *Media Psychology, 4*, 355–380.

Faul, F., & Erdfelder, E. (1992). GPOWER: A priori, post-hoc, and compromise power analysis for MS-DOS [Computer program]. Bonn, FRG: Bonn University, Department of Psychology.

Ferguson, D. A., & Perse, E. M. (2000). The World Wide Web as a functional alternative to television. *Journal of Broadcasting & Electronic Media, 44*, 155–174.

Fredin, E. S., & David, P. (1998). Browsing and the hypermedia interaction cycle: A model of self-efficacy and goal dynamics. *Journalism and Mass Communication Quarterly, 75*, 35–54.

Gabbard, R. B. (2000). Constructivism, hypermedia, and the World Wide Web. *CyberPsychology & Behavior, 3*, 103–110.

Glanzer, M. (1972). Storage mechanisms in recall. In G. H. Bower (Ed.), *The psychology of learning and motivation: Advances in research and theory* (pp. 129–193). New York: Academic Press.

Guay, F., Vallerand, R. J., & Blanchard, C. (2000). On the assessment of situational intrinsic and extrinsic motivation: The Situational Motivation Scale (SIMS). *Motivation and Emotion, 24,* 175–213.

Hartley, K. (2001). Learning strategies and hypermedia instruction. *Journal of Educational Multimedia & Hypermedia, 10,* 285–305.

Hess, B. (1999). Graduate student cognition during information retrieval using the World Wide Web: A pilot study. *Computers & Education, 33,* 1–13.

Horney, M. (1993). A measure of hypertext linearity. *Journal of Educational Multimedia and Hypermedia, 2,* 67–82.

Howes, A., & Payne, S. (1990). Display-based competence: Towards user models for menu-driven interfaces. *International Journal of Man-Machine Studies, 33,* 637–655.

Hull, C. L. (1943). *Principles of behavior.* New York: Appleton-Century-Drofts.

———. (1951). *Essentials of behavior.* New Haven, Connecticut: Yale University Press.

Humphreys, M. S., & Revelle, W. (1984). Personality, motivation, and performance: A theory of the relationship between individual differences and information processing. *Psychological Review, 91,* 153–184.

Izawa, C. (1999). On human memory: A brief introduction. In C. Izawa (Ed.), *On human memory: Evolution, progress, and reflections on the 30th anniversary of the Atkinson–Shiffrin model* (pp. 1–15). New Jersey: Erlbaum.

Jonassen, D. H. (1988). Designing structured hypertext and structuring access to hypertext. *Educational Technology, 28,* 13–16.

———. (1992). Designing hypertext for learning. In E. Scanlon, & T. O'Shea (Eds.), *New directions in educational technology* (pp. 123–130). Berlin: Springer-Verlag.

———. (1993). Effects of semantically structured hypertext knowledge bases on users' knowledge structures. In C. McKnight, A. Dillon, & J. Richardson (Eds.), *Hypertext: A psychological perspective* (pp. 153–167). West Sussex, England: Ellis Horwood.

Jonassen, D. H., Beissner, K., & Yacci, M. (1993). *Structural knowledge: Techniques for representing, conveying, and acquiring structural knowledge.* Hillsdale, New Jersey: Erlbaum.

Jonassen, D. H., Hernandez-Serrano, J., & Choi, I. (2000). Integrating constructivism and learning technologies. In J. M. Spector, & T. M. Anderson (Eds.),

*Integrated and holistic perspectives on learning, instruction and technology: Understanding complexity* (pp. 103–128). Dordrecht, The Netherlands: Kluwer Academic Publishers.

Jonassen, D. H., & Mandl, H. (1989). *Designing hypermedia for learning.* Berlin: Springer-Verlag.

Jonassen, D. H., & Wang, S. (1993). Acquiring structural knowledge from semantically structured hypertext. *Journal of computer-based instruction, 20,* 1–8.

Joo, Y, Bong, M., & Choi, H. (2000). Self-efficacy for self-regulated learning, academic self-efficacy, and Internet self-efficacy in web-based Instruction. *ETR & D: Educational Technology Research & Development, 48*(2), 5–17.

Kalichman, S. C., Benotsch, E. G., Weinhardt, L., Austin, J., Luke, W., & Cherry, C. (2003). Health-related Internet use, coping, social support, and health indicators in people living with HIV / AIDS: Preliminary results from a community survey. *Health Psychology, 22,* 111–116.

Kalichman, S. C., Weinhardt, L., Benotsch, E., DiFonzo, K., Luke W., & Austin, J. (2002). Internet access and Internet use for health information among people living with HIV-AIDS. *Patient Education and Counseling, 46*(2), 109–116.

Kalyuga, S., Chandler, P., Tuovinen, J., & Sweller, J. (2001). When problem solving is superior to studying worked examples. *Journal of Educational Psychology, 93,* 579–588.

Kardash, C. M., & Amlund, J. T. (1991). Self-reported learning strategies and learning from expository text. *Contemporary Educational Psychology, 16,* 117–138.

Katz, E., Blumler, J. G., & Gurevitch, M. (1974). Utilization of mass communication by the individual. In J. G. Blumler, & E. Katz (Eds.), *The uses of mass communications: Current perspectives on gratifications research* (pp. 19–32). Beverly Hills, California: Sage.

Kettanurak, V., Ramamuthy, K., & Haseman, W. D. (2001). User attitude as a mediator of learning performance improvement in an interactive multimedia environment: An empirical investigation of the degree of interactivity and learning styles. *International Journal of Human-Computer Studies, 54,* 541–583.

Kitajima, M., & Polson, P. G. (1995). A comprehension-based model of correct performance and errors in skilled, display-based, human-computer interaction. *International Journal of Human-Computer Studies, 43,* 65–99.

Lachman, R., Lachman, J. L., & Butterfield, E. C. (1979). *Cognitive psychology and information processing: An introduction.* New Jersey: Erlbaum.

Lang, A. (2000). The limited capacity model of mediated message processing. *Journal of Communication, 50*(1), 46–70.

LaRose, R., Mastro, D., & Eastin, M. S. (2001). Understanding Internet usage: A social-cognitive approach to uses and gratifications. *Social Science Computer Review, 19*, 395–413.

Lee, M. J., & Tedder, M. C. (2003). The effects of three different computer texts on readers' recall: Based on working memory capacity. *Computers in Human Behavior, 19*, 767–783.

Leung, A. C. K. (2003). Providing navigation aids and online learning helps to support user control: A conceptual model on computer-based learning. *Journal of Computer Information Systems, 43*, 10–17.

Macedo-Rouet, M., Rouet, J-F., Epstein, I., & Fayard, P. (2003). Effects of online reading on popular science comprehension. *Science Communication, 25*, 99–128.

MacGregor, S. K. (1999). Hypermedia navigation profiles: Cognitive characteristics and information processing strategies. *Journal of Educational Computing Research, 20*, 189–206.

McDonald, S., & Stevenson, R. J. (1996). Disorientation in hypertext: The effects of three text structures on navigation performance. *Applied Ergonomics, 27*, 61–68.

———. (1998a). Effects of text structure and prior knowledge of the learner on navigation in hypertext. *Human Factors, 40*, 18–27.

———. (1998b). Navigation in hyperspace: An evaluation of the effects of navigational tools and subject matter expertise on browsing and information retrieval in hypertext. *Interacting with Computers, 10*, 129–142.

Melton, A. W. (1963). Implications of short-term memory for a general theory of memory. *Journal of Verbal Learning and Verbal Behavior, 2*, 1–21.

Midgley, C., Maehr, M., Hruda, L. Z., Anderman, E., Anderman, L., Freeman, K. E., et al. (2000). *Manual for the patterns of adaptive learning scales.* http://www.umich.edu/~pals/pals/PALS%202000_V12Word97.pdf  Retrieved March 16, 2004.

Miller, G. A. (1956). The magical number seven, plus or minus two: Some limits on our capacity for processing information. *The Psychological Review, 63*, 81–97.

Morgan, W. (2002). Heterotropes: Learning the rhetoric of hyperlinks. *Education, Communication & Information, 2*, 215–233.

Morton, J. (1970). A functional model for memory. In D. A. Norman (Ed.), *Models of human memory* (pp. 203–254). New York: Academic Press.

Murdock, B. B., Jr. (1972). Short-term memory. In G. H. Bower (Ed.), *The psychology of learning and motivation: Advances in research and theory* (pp. 67–127). New York: Academic Press.

————. (1982). A theory for the storage and retrieval of item and associative information. *Psychological Review, 89*, 609–626.

————. (1999). The buffer 30 years later: Working memory in a Theory of Distributed Associative Memory (TODAM). In C. Izawa (Ed.), *On human memory: Evolution, progress, and reflections on the 30th anniversary of the Atkinson–Shiffrin model* (pp. 35–57). New Jersey: Erlbaum.

Nilsson, R. M., & Mayer, R. E. (2002). The effects of graphic organizers giving cues to the structure of a hypertext document on users' navigation strategies and performance. *International Journal of Human-Computer Studies, 57*, 1–26.

Novak, J. D. (1990), Concept mapping: A useful tool for science education. *Journal of Research in Science Teaching, 27*, 937–949.

Novak, J. D., & Gowin, D. B. (1984). *Learning how to learn*. London: Cambridge University Press.

Paas, F. G. W. C. (1992). Training strategies for attaining transfer of problem-solving skill in statistics: A cognitive-load approach. *Journal of Educational Psychology, 84*, 429–434.

Paas, F. G. W. C., van Merriënboer, J. J. G., & Adam, J. J. (1994). Measurement of cognitive load in instructional research. *Perceptual and Motor Skills, 79*, 419–430.

Palmer, D. J., & Goetz, T. (1988). Selection and use of study strategies: The role of the studier's beliefs about self and strategies. In C. E. Weinstein, E. T. Goetz, & P. A. Alexander (Eds.), *Learning and study strategies: Issues in assessment, instruction, and evaluation* (pp. 41–61). San Diego: Academic.

Papacharissi, Z., & Rubin, A. M. (2000). Predictors of Internet use. *Journal of Broadcasting & Electronic Media, 44*, 175–196.

Postman, L. (1964). Short-term memory and incidental learning. In A. W. Melton (Ed.), *Categories of human learning* (pp. 145–201). New York: Academic Press.

Potelle, H., & Rouet, J-F. (2003). Effects of content representation and readers' prior knowledge on the comprehension of hypertext. *International Journal of Human-Computer Studies, 58*, 327–345.

Qiu, L. (1993). Markov models of search state patterns in a hypertext information retrieval system. *Journal of the American Society for Information Science, 44*, 413–427.

Quillian, M. R. (1968). Semantic memory. In M. Minsky (Ed.), *Semantic information processing* (pp. 227–270). Cambridge, Massachusetts: Massachusetts Institute of Technology.

Raaijmakers, J. G. W., & Shiffrin, R. M. (1981). Search of associative memory. *Psychological Review, 88*, 93–134.

Royer, J. M., Cisero, C. A., & Carlo, M. S. (1993). Techniques and procedures for assessing cognitive skills. *Review of Educational Research, 63*, 201–243.

Rubin, A. M. (1983). Television uses and gratifications: The interactions of viewing patterns and motivations. *Journal of Broadcasting, 27*, 37–52.

———. (1984). Ritualized and instrumental television viewing. *Journal of Communication, 34*(3), 67–77.

Schmek, R. R. (1983). Learning styles of college students. In R. F. Dillon, & R. R. Schmeck (Eds.). *Individual Differences in Cognition* (Vol. 1) (pp. 233–279). New York: Academic.

———. (1988). Individual differences and learning strategies. In C. E. Weinstein, E. T. Goetz, & P. A. Alexander (Eds.), *Learning and study strategies: Issues in assessment, instruction, and evaluation* (pp. 171–191). San Diego: Academic.

Schmek, R. R., Geisler-Brenstein, E., & Cercy, S. P. (1991). Self-concept and learning: The revised inventory of learning processes. *Educational Psychology, 11*(3–4), 343–362.

Schmek, R. R., Ribich, F., & Ramanaiah, N. (1977). Development of a self-report inventory for assessing individual differences in learning processes. *Applied Psychological Measurement, 1*, 413–431.

Schunk, D. H. (2000). *Learning theories: An educational perspective* (3rd ed.). New Jersey: Prentice Hall.

Scott, J. (1991). *Social network analysis: A handbook*. Thousand Oaks, California: Sage.

Seifert, T. L. (1993). Effects of elaborative interrogation with prose passages. *Journal of Educational Psychology, 85*, 642–651.

Shiffrin, R. M., & Atkinson, R. C. (1969). Storage and retrieval processes in long-term memory. *Psychological Review, 76*, 179–193.

Sinclair, K. J., Renshaw C. E., & Taylor, H. A. (2004). Improving computer-assisted instruction in teaching higher-order skills. *Computers & Education, 42*, 169–180.

Sperling, G. (1960). The information available in brief visual presentations. *Psychological Monographs, 74*, 1–29.

Steinberg, E. R. (1989). Cognition and learner control: A literature review, 1977–1988. *Journal of Computer-Based Instruction, 16*, 117–121.

Sweller, J. (1988). Cognitive load during problem solving: Effects on learning. *Cognitive Science, 12*, 257–285.

Sweller, J. Chandler, P., Tierney, P., & Cooper, M. (1990). Cognitive load as a factor in the structuring of technical material. *Journal of Experimental Psychology: General, 119*, 176–192.

Tewksbury, D., & Althaus, S. L. (2000). Differences in knowledge acquisition among readers of the paper and online versions of a national newspaper. *Journalism & Mass Communication Quarterly, 77*, 457–479.

Thompson, L. F., Meriac, J. P., & Cope, J. G. (2002). Motivating online performance: The influences of goal setting and Internet self-efficacy. *Social Science Computer Review, 20*, 149–160.

Torkzadeh, G., & van Dyke, T. P. (2001). Development and validation of an Internet self-efficacy scale. *Behaviour & Information Technology, 20*, 275–280.

Tremayne, M., & Dunwoody, S. (2001). Interactivity, information processing, and learning on the World Wide Web. *Science Communication, 23*, 111–134.

Tulving, E. (1972). Episodic and semantic memory. In E. Tulving & W. Donaldson (Eds.), *Organization of memory* (pp. 381–403). New York: Academic Press.

Tulving, E., & Osler, S. (1968). Effectiveness of retrieval cues in memory for words. *Journal of Experimental Psychology, 77*, 593–601.

Tulving, E., & Patterson, R. D. (1968). Functional units and retrieval processes in free recall. *Journal of Experimental Psychology, 77*, 239–248.

Tulving, E., & Pearlstone, Z. (1966). Availability versus accessibility of information in memory for words. *Journal of Verbal Learning and Learning Behavior, 5*, 381–391.

Tulving, E., & Thomson, D. M. (1973). Encoding specificity and retrieval processes in episodic memory. *Psychological Review, 80*, 352–373.

Unz, D. C., & Hesse, F. W. (1999). The use of hypertext for learning. *Journal of Educational Computing Research, 20*, 279–295.

Vallerand, R. J., & Ratelle, C. F. (2002). Intrinsic and extrinsic motivation: A hierarchical model. In E. L. Deci, & R. M. Ryan (Eds.), *Handbook of self-determination research* (pp. 37–63). Rochester, New York: The University of Rochester Press.

Wang, A. Y., & Newlin, M. H. (2002). Predictors of web-student performance: The role of self-efficacy and reasons for taking an on-line class. *Computers in Human Behavior, 18*, 151–163.

Wasserman, S., & Faust, K. (1994). *Social network analysis: Methods and applications*. Cambridge, UK: Cambridge Press.

Waugh, N. C., & Norman, D. A. (1965). Primary memory. *Psychological Review, 72*, 89–104.

Weiner, B. (1992). *Human motivation: Metaphors, theories, and research.* Newbury Park: Sage.

Weinstein, C. E., Zimmermann, S. A., & Palmer, D. R. (1988). Assessing learning strategies: The design and development of the LASSI. In C. E. Weinstein, E. T. Goetz, & P. A. Alexander (Eds.), *Learning and study strategies: Issues in assessment, instruction, and evaluation* (pp. 25–40). San Diego: Academic.

West, R. L., & Thorn, R. M. (2001). Goal-setting, self-efficacy, and memory performance in older and younger adults. *Experimental Aging Research, 27,* 41–65.

# Name Index

Adam, J. J., 56
Althaus, S. L., 20
Amlund, J. T., 13
Ashman, H., 18
Astleitner, H., 15
Atkinson, R. C., 7, 8

Balasubramanian, V., 18
Bandura, A., 1, 2, 3, 38
Bantz, C. R., 36
Barab, S. A., 17
Beissner, K., 11
Bieber, M., 17, 18
Blanchard, C., 36
Blumler, J. G., 36
Bong, M., 54, 94
Brown, A. L., 37, 38
Butterfield, E. C., 7

Calisir, F., 20
Cameron, J., 36
Campbell, D., 103, 112
Carlo, M. S., 38
Carmel, E., 32
Cassell, M. M., 1
Cercy, S. P., 13
Chandler, P., 40, 56
Charney, T., 54, 127, 148
Chen, H., 32
Chen, P., 30
Cheuvront, B., 1
Choi, H., 54
Choi, I., 5
Cisero, C. A., 38
Clariana, R. B., 14
Cohen, J., 51
Cooper, M., 40
Cope, J. G., 39

Cortese, J., 14, 15, 20, 26, 28–31, 57, 58, 89, 90, 93, 102, 117
Cozijn, R., xxv
Craik, F. I. M., 10, 13, 14, 29
Cress, U., 25, 29, 30, 88, 89

David, P., 39
de Jong, T., 24, 26, 28, 31, 51, 90
Deci, E. L., 36, 37
Dunwoody, S., 13, 14, 20, 24, 26, 29, 30, 34, 37, 41, 54, 56, 92, 130

Eastin, M. S., 54, 127, 148
Eisenberger, R., 36
Entwistle, N., 13
Epstein, I., 41
Erdfelder, E., 51
Ertmer, P. A., 5, 21, 22, 23
Estes, W. K., 9, 10
Eveland, W. P., Jr., 13–15, 20, 24, 26, 28–31, 34, 37, 41, 54, 56–58, 87, 89, 90, 92, 93, 102, 117, 130

Fajen, B. R., 17
Faul, F., 51
Faust, K., 58
Fayard, P., 41
Ferguson, D. A., 36
Fredin, E. S., 39

Gabbard R. B., 23, 24
Geisler-Brenstein, E., 13
Glanzer, M., 7
Goetz, T., 37, 38
Goldsmith, T. E., xxvi
Gowin, D. B., 16
Greenberg, B. S., 54, 127, 148
Guay, F., 36, 55, 130, 159

Gurel, Z., 20
Gurevitch, M., 36

Hartley, K., 93
Haseman, W. D., 22
Hernandez-Serrano, J., 5
Hess, B., 6
Hesse, F. W., 34
Hocevar, D., 94
Horney, M., 18
Howes, A., 34, 92
Hull, C. L., 35
Humphreys, M. S., 37

Izawa, C., 7

Jackson, C., 1
Jonassen, D. H., 5, 11, 12, 14–18, 21,
    23, 24, 26–30, 89, 90, 91, 93, 102,
    115, 118–120
Joo, Y., 54, 94, 127, 148

Kalichman, S. C., 1
Kalyuga, S., 56, 130
Kardash, C. M., 13
Katz, E., 36
Kettanurak, V., 22, 23
Kitajima, M., 34
Knabel, O. B., 25, 29, 30, 88, 89
Kulikowich, J. M., 17

Lachman, J. L., 7–10, 122
Lachman, R., 7–10, 122
Lang, A., 10–12
LaRose, R., 54, 127, 148
Lee, D., 14
Lee, M. J., xxvi, 26
Leung, A. C. K., 30
Leutner, D., 15
Lockhart, R. S., 10, 13, 14, 29

Macedo-Rouet, M., 41, 96
MacGregor, S. K., 32, 91
Maes, A., xxv, xxvi
Mandl, H., 18
Marton, K., 15, 20, 26, 28–31, 57,
    58, 87, 89, 102, 117
Mastro, D., 54, 127, 148
Mayer, R. E., 25
McDonald, S., 19, 20, 25, 32
McGrath, D., 30
Melton, A. W., 7
Meriac, J. P., 39
Midgley, C., 54, 127, 148
Miller, G. A., 7
Morgan, W., 30, 88
Morton, J., 10
Murdock, B. B., Jr., 10

Newby, T. J., 5, 21–23
Newlin, M. H., 39, 40, 94
Nilsson, R. M., 25
Norman, D. A., 7
Novak, J. D., 16

Oinas-Kukkonen, H., 18
Osler, S., 9, 13, 121

Paas, F. G. W. C., 56, 130, 159
Palmer, D. J., 37, 38
Palmer, D. R., 13
Papacharissi, Z., 36
Park, H., 14
Patterson, R. D., 10, 13
Payne, S., 34, 92
Pearlstone, Z., 9, 121
Pelletier, L. G., 36
Perse, E. M., 36
Polson P. G., 34
Postman, L., 6
Potelle, H., 20

Qiu, L., 33
Quillian, M. R., 6

Raaijmakers, J. G. W., 9
Ramamuthy, K., 22
Ramanaiah, N., 13
Ratelle, C. F., 36
Renshaw C. E., 41
Revelle, W., 37
Ribich, F., 13
Rouet, J-F., 20, 41
Royer, J. M., 38
Rubin, A. M., 36
Ryan, R. M., 36, 37

Schmek, R. R., 13
Schunk, D. H., 5, 13, 90
Scott, J., 58
Seifert, T. L., 13, 14, 29
Seo, M., 15, 20
Shiffrin, R. M., 7–9
Sinclair, K. J., 41
Sperling, G., 6
Stanley, J., 103, 112
Steinberg, E. R., 32
Stephen, C., 32
Stevenson, R. J., 19, 20, 25, 32
Sweller, J., 40, 56

Taylor, H. A., 41
Tedder, M. C., xxvi, 26
Tewksbury, D., 20
Thompson, L. F., 39
Thomson, D. M., 11, 13

Thorn, R. M., 39
Tierney, P., 40
Torkzadeh, G., 54, 127, 148
Tremayne, M., 30
Trumpower, D. L., xxvi
Tulving, E., 6, 9–11, 13, 121
Tuovinen, J., 56

Unz, D. C., 34

Vallerand, R. J., 36
van der Hulst, A., 24, 26, 28, 31, 51, 90
van Dyke, T. P., 54, 127, 148
van Geel, A., xxv
van Merriënboer, J. J. G., 56
Vitali, F., 18

Wang, A. Y., 39, 40, 94
Wang, S., 26–30, 89, 93, 102, 118
Wasserman, S., 58
Waterston, S., 13
Waugh, N. C., 7
Weiner, B., 35
Weinstein, C. E., 13
West, R. L., 39

Xie, G., xxvi

Yacci, M., 11
Young, M. F., 17

Zimmermann, S. A., 13

# SUBJECT INDEX

Alternative medicine, xx, 42, 46, 53, 86, 90, 91, 105, 107, 113, 127, 136, 142, 149
Array Model, 10
Atkinson-Joula theory, 8
Atkinson-Shiffrin model, 7

Behaviorism, 5, 21, 22

Card sort, 15, 28
Cognitive load, 40–43, 46, 53, 56, 74, 77, 79, 85, 86, 95, 96, 99, 102, 105, 107, 108, 110, 114–116, 118, 119, 130, 159
   Cognitive Load – effort, 56, 57, 60, 74, 75, 78, 79, 81–83, 86, 95, 98, 99, 108, 110, 111, 119–121, 123
   Cognitive Load – misunderstanding, 56, 57, 60, 74, 76–79, 82, 83, 95, 97–99, 108, 122, 123
Cognitive Load Theory, 40, 96, 97, 123
Cognitivism, 22, 23
Composite Holographic Associative Recall Model, 10
Concept maps, 15–17
Constructivism, 22, 23
Covert cognitive processes, 13
Cued recall, 14, 42

Deep processing, 13, 29
Definitional elaboration site, 32–35, 41–43, 45, 47, 60, 62, 63, 65–67, 69, 74, 79, 118, 121
Depth of processing, 10
Drive theory, 35

Elaboration, 3, 4, 13, 14, 29, 30, 31, 87, 88, 90, 93, 96, 98, 99, 101, 102, 119, 123
Elaborative interrogation, 13, 29
Elaborative processing, 13
Encoding, 4, 6, 10, 11, 23, 42, 121
Encoding specificity, 9, 121

Feedback, 2, 22, 39
Finite-State Decision model, 10
Free recall, 9, 14, 20, 102

Generative learning, 27
Graphic organizers, 15

Health communication, 1
Hierarchical structure, 19, 42
Human agency, 3, 32, 38
Hypertext, 17, 18, 21, 33
Hypertext Interaction Cycle (HIC), 39
Hypertext links, 30, 45

Incidental learning, 6
Information processing, xx, xxii, 10, 11, 13
Interactive multimedia instruction (IMI), 22

Knowledge, 4, 5, 12–15, 20, 25, 26, 29, 31, 32, 43, 86, 88, 90, 91, 118, 119, 122
   Configural knowledge, 28
   Declarative knowledge, 12
   Definitional knowledge, 28, 33, 34, 38, 40, 41, 43, 46, 53, 57, 59, 60–63, 65–70, 72–77, 79–82, 85, 86, 88–92, 95–101, 118, 121–123

Factual knowledge, 24, 26, 30–33, 35, 38, 40, 42, 43, 46, 53, 57, 59, 60, 61, 63, 64, 66, 67, 69, 71, 74, 79, 82, 83, 86, 88–90, 92, 95, 96, 101, 121, 123
Knowledge structure, xxi, xxii, xxv, xxvi, 12, 14–17, 20, 21, 24–28, 30, 31, 33, 34, 38, 40–43, 46, 53, 58–61, 63–66, 68–73, 77, 78, 82, 83, 86, 89–93, 95–97, 100–105, 107–123, 130–136, 149–157, 159–165
Procedural knowledge, 12
Propositional knowledge, 28
Knowledge gap hypothesis, xxi

Learner control, 22
Levels of processing approach, 10
Limited capacity model, 10, 13
Linear, xxvi, xxvii, 19–21, 24–26, 33, 89, 92
Linear Association Model, 10
Logogen model, 10

Matched Filters, 10
Matrix, 10
Meaning making, 4, 10, 12, 22–24
Memory, xxv, xxvii, 4, 6, 7, 9, 10, 13, 14, 29, 39
Analogue memory, 9
Episodic memory, 6
Iconic memory, 6
Long-term memory, 4, 7–9, 11, 12
Long-term store, 7, 8
Primary memory, 7
Secondary memory, 7
Semantic memory, 6, 8, 11
Short-term memory, 7, 9, 11
Short-term store, 7
Working memory, xxvii, 8
Metacognition, 38
MINERVA, 10

MINERVA2, 10
Motivation, xxi, xxii, 2–4, 14, 35–39, 42, 43, 46, 53, 55, 60, 69, 70–72, 81–83, 86, 92, 93, 103, 105, 107, 110, 114, 116, 122, 130, 159
Extrinsic motivation, 36, 37
Intrinsic motivation, 36–38, 55, 56, 69–71, 93, 108, 116
Multi-store model, 7, 9, 10

Nonlinear, xxvi, 18–20, 23–26, 28, 30–35, 41, 42, 45, 47, 62, 63, 65, 67, 68, 74, 77, 78, 89, 92, 102, 103, 105, 110, 114, 117

Pathfinder networks, 16, 17
Pop-up windows, xx, xxv, xxvi, 27, 29–31, 42, 45, 47, 87–91, 94, 96–100, 118
Prior knowledge, 20, 32

Rehearsal buffer, 8
Relational elaboration site, 32–35, 41–43, 45, 47, 60, 62, 63, 65, 66, 68, 69, 77, 79
Resonance, 10
Resonance-Retrieval Model, 10
Retrieval, 2–6, 8–14, 23, 28, 42, 121

Schema theory, 11, 21
Search of Associative Memory model, 9
Self-determinism theory, 37
Self-efficacy, 4, 38, 40
Internet self-efficacy, 43, 72–74, 94, 95
Semantic maps, 15
Semantic networks, 21, 27
Sensory register, 7, 8
Shiffrin-Schneider theory, 8
Similarity ratings, 15
Situational Motivation Scale, 55

Social cognitive theory, 2–4, 42

Solomon Four-Group Design, xxii, 103, 104, 110, 112, 116, 117

Spider maps, 15

Spreading-Activation theory, 10

Storage, 4–13, 23, 42

Subject expertise, 2, 4, 32–35, 42, 43, 46, 53, 60, 64–67, 79, 80, 82, 86, 90, 91, 96, 97, 102, 105, 107, 108, 110, 111, 114–116, 118, 119, 121, 122, 127, 149

Synthesis-analysis, 13

Theory of Distributed Associative Memory, 10

Tree construction tasks, 15

Uses and gratifications, 35–37

Web expertise, 4, 33–35, 42, 43, 46, 53–55, 60, 67–69, 81–83, 86, 91, 92, 98, 102, 105, 107, 108, 110, 111, 114–116, 122, 126, 148

Word association proximities, 15

Printed in the United States
83528LV00004B/15/A

9 781934 043134